AINS 23 Course Guide

Commercial Insurance
4th Edition

The Institutes
720 Providence Road, Suite 100
Malvern, Pennsylvania 19355-3433

4th Edition • 1st Printing • October 2014

ISBN 978-0-89463-789-6

Contents

 ## Study Materials Available for AINS 23

Commercial Insurance, 4th ed., 2014, AICPCU.

AINS 23 *Course Guide,* 4th ed., 2014, AICPCU (includes access code for SMART Online Practice Exams).

AINS 23 SMART Study Aids—Review Notes and Flash Cards, 4th ed.

The CPCU Handbook of Insurance Policies, AICPCU.

Student Resources

Catalog A complete listing of our offerings can be found in The Institutes' professional development catalog, including information about:

- Current programs and courses
- Current textbooks, course guides, SMART Study Aids, and online offerings
- Program completion requirements
- Exam registration

To obtain a copy of the catalog, visit our website at www.TheInstitutes.org or contact Customer Service at (800) 644-2101.

How to Prepare for Institutes Exams This free handbook is designed to help you by:

- Giving you ideas on how to use textbooks and course guides as effective learning tools
- Providing steps for answering exam questions effectively
- Recommending exam-day strategies

The handbook is printable from the Student Services Center on The Institutes' website at www.TheInstitutes.org or available by calling Customer Service at (800) 644-2101.

Educational Counseling Services To ensure that you take courses matching both your needs and your skills, you can obtain free counseling from The Institutes by:

- Emailing your questions to advising@TheInstitutes.org
- Calling an Institutes' counselor directly at (610) 644-2100, ext. 7601
- Obtaining and completing a self-inventory form, available on our website at www.TheInstitutes.org or by contacting Customer Service at (800) 644-2101

Exam Registration Information As you proceed with your studies, be sure to arrange for your exam.

- Visit our website at www.TheInstitutes.org/forms to access and print the Registration Booklet, which contains information and forms needed to register for your exam.
- Plan to register with The Institutes well in advance of your exam.

How to Contact The Institutes For more information on any of these publications and services:

- Visit our website at www.TheInstitutes.org
- Call us at (800) 644-2101 or (610) 644-2100 outside the U.S.
- Email us at customerservice@TheInstitutes.org
- Fax us at (610) 640-9576
- Write to us at The Institutes, Customer Service, 720 Providence Road, Suite 100, Malvern, PA 19355-3433

Using This Course Guide

This course guide will help you learn the course content and prepare for the exam.

Each assignment in this course guide typically includes the following components:

Educational Objectives These are the most important study tools in the course guide. Because all of the questions on the exam are based on the Educational Objectives, the best way to study for the exam is to focus on these objectives.

Each Educational Objective typically begins with one of the following action words, which indicate the level of understanding required for the exam:

Analyze—Determine the nature and the relationship of the parts.

Apply—Put to use for a practical purpose.

Associate—Bring together into relationship.

Calculate—Determine numeric values by mathematical process.

Classify—Arrange or organize according to class or category.

Compare—Show similarities and differences.

Contrast—Show only differences.

Define—Give a clear, concise meaning.

Describe—Represent or give an account.

Determine—Settle or decide.

Evaluate—Determine the value or merit.

Explain—Relate the importance or application.

Identify or list—Name or make a list.

Illustrate—Give an example.

Justify—Show to be right or reasonable.

Paraphrase—Restate in your own words.

Recommend—Suggest or endorse something to be used.

Summarize—Concisely state the main points.

Outline The outline lists the topics in the assignment. Read the outline before the required reading to become familiar with the assignment content and the relationships of topics.

Key Words and Phrases These words and phrases are fundamental to understanding the assignment and have a common meaning for those working in insurance. After completing the required reading, test your understanding of the assignment's Key Words and Phrases by writing their definitions.

Review Questions The review questions test your understanding of what you have read. Review the Educational Objectives and required reading, then answer the questions to the best of your ability. When you are finished, check the answers at the end of the assignment to evaluate your comprehension.

Application Questions These questions continue to test your knowledge of the required reading by applying what you've studied to "hypothetical" real-life situations. Again, check the suggested answers at the end of the assignment to review your progress.

Sample Exam Your course guide includes a sample exam (located at the back) or a code for accessing SMART Online Practice Exams (which appears on the inside of the cover). Use the option available for the course you're taking to become familiar with the test format.

For courses that offer SMART Online Practice Exams, you can either download and print a sample credentialing exam or take full practice exams using questions like those that will appear on your credentialing exam. SMART Online Practice Exams are as close as you can get to experiencing an actual exam before taking one.

More Study Aids

The Institutes also produce supplemental study tools, called SMART Study Aids, for many of our courses. When SMART Study Aids are available for a course, they are listed on page iii of the course guide. SMART Study Aids include Review Notes and Flash Cards and are excellent tools to help you learn and retain the information in each assignment.

A

Direct Your Learning

Commercial Property Insurance, Part I

Educational Objectives

After learning the content of this assignment, you should be able to:

1. Describe commercial property insurance in terms of these elements:
   - The major categories of loss exposures that can be covered
   - The components of a commercial property coverage part

2. Determine whether a described item of property qualifies as Covered Property under one or more of these categories in the Building and Personal Property Coverage Form:
   - Building
   - Your Business Personal Property
   - Personal Property of Others

3. Determine which of the additional coverages and coverage extensions of the Building and Personal Property Coverage Form (BPP) apply to a described loss.

4. Determine whether the cause of a described loss is a covered cause of loss under either the Causes of Loss—Basic Form or the Causes of Loss—Broad Form.

5. Determine whether the cause of a described loss is a Covered Cause of Loss under the Causes of Loss—Special Form.

6. Apply the Limits of Insurance and Deductible provisions of the Building and Personal Property Coverage Form to a described loss.

Outline

▶ **Overview of Commercial Property Insurance**
  A. Commercial Property Loss Exposures
    1. Types of Property
    2. Causes of Loss to Property
    3. Financial Consequences of Property Losses
  B. Components of a Commercial Property Coverage Part
    1. Commercial Property Declarations
    2. Commercial Property Coverage Forms
    3. Causes of Loss Forms
    4. Commercial Property Conditions
    5. Endorsements
▶ **BPP Covered Property**
  A. Categories of Covered Property
    1. Building
    2. Your Business Personal Property
    3. Personal Property of Others
  B. Property Not Covered
▶ **BPP Additional Coverages and Coverage Extensions**
  A. Additional Coverages
    1. Debris Removal
    2. Preservation of Property
    3. Fire Department Service Charge
    4. Pollutant Cleanup and Removal
    5. Increased Cost of Construction
    6. Electronic Data
  B. Coverage Extensions
    1. Newly Acquired or Constructed Property
    2. Personal Effects and Property of Others
    3. Valuable Papers and Records (Other Than Electronic Data)
    4. Property Off-Premises
    5. Outdoor Property
    6. Non-Owned Detached Trailers
    7. Business Personal Property Temporarily in Portable Storage Units

▶ **Causes of Loss—Basic Form and Broad Form**
  A. Covered Causes of Loss
  B. Exclusions
    1. Ordinance or Law
    2. Earth Movement
    3. Governmental Action
    4. Nuclear Hazard
    5. Utility Services
    6. War and Military Action
    7. Water
    8. "Fungus," Wet Rot, Dry Rot, and Bacteria
    9. Other Exclusions
  C. Additional Coverages
▶ **Causes of Loss—Special Form**
  A. Exclusions and Limitations
    1. Exclusions and Limitations Unique to the Special Form
    2. Theft-Related Exclusions and Limitations
  B. Additional Coverages and Coverage Extensions
▶ **BPP Limits of Insurance and Deductible**
  A. Limits of Insurance
  B. Deductible

s.m.a.r.t.® tips Don't spend time on material you have already mastered. The SMART Review Notes are organized by the Educational Objectives found in each assignment to help you track your study.

For each assignment, you should define or describe each of the Key Words and Phrases and answer each of the Review and Application Questions.

Educational Objective 1

Describe commercial property insurance in terms of these elements:

- **The major categories of loss exposures that can be covered**
- **The components of a commercial property coverage part**

Key Words and Phrases

Real property (realty)

Personal property

Commercial property coverage part

Commercial package policy (CPP)

Monoline policy

Package modification factors

Commercial property declarations page

Commercial property coverage form

Causes of loss form

Commercial Property Conditions

Review Questions

1-1. What are the components of a commercial property loss exposure?

1-2. Contrast real property and personal property.

1-3. Identify the classifications into which personal property falls for insurance purposes.

1-4. Explain how a cause of loss affects property.

1-5. Identify the three main adverse financial consequences of property loss exposures.

1-6. Identify the components of a commercial property coverage part.

1-7. What information is contained on a commercial property declarations page that pertains specifically to property insurance?

1-8. Identify the typical elements of a commercial property coverage form.

1-9. Identify the three types of causes of loss forms.

Educational Objective 2

Determine whether a described item of property qualifies as Covered Property under one or more of these categories in the Building and Personal Property Coverage Form:

- **Building**
- **Your Business Personal Property**
- **Personal Property of Others**

Review Questions

2-1. Identify the three broad categories of property covered by the Building and Personal Property Coverage Form, also referred to as the BPP.

2-2. What elements are included in the BPP's definition of Building?

2-3. In order to be insured under the BPP, where must Your Business Personal Property be located?

2-4. Identify a potential negative consequence of ignoring improvements and betterments when setting the amount of insurance that a tenant should carry.

2-5. What is the purpose of coverage for Personal Property of Others?

2-6. Identify reasons why the BPP excludes some kinds of property from coverage.

Application Question

2-7. A used celebrity guitar business conducts most of its sales via its website. Its warehouse and office operations are housed in a large building, which is insured under a BPP. The office contains the company's servers, currently valued at $300,000. Two years ago, the company purchased a separate electronic data processing (EDP) equipment policy to cover its computer hardware. The company has kept the policy in force, but it has not increased the original $200,000 amount of insurance. A computer room fire destroys all of its servers. How much will each policy provide in covering the loss?

Educational Objective 3

Determine which of the additional coverages and coverage extensions of the Building and Personal Property Coverage Form (BPP) apply to a described loss.

Review Questions

3-1. Identify the three methods an insured can use to increase the limit of insurance for the Building and Personal Property Coverage Form, also referred to as the BPP.

3-2. Explain the purpose of the BPP's Debris Removal additional coverage.

3-3. Identify the circumstance under which the BPP's Preservation of Property additional coverage covers property.

3-4. Explain the purpose of the BPP's Pollutant Cleanup and Removal additional coverage.

3-5. Identify why the BPP excludes electronic data in most instances except as provided by the Electronic Data additional coverage.

Application Question

3-6.   An office building and its contents are insured under a Commercial Package Policy that includes the BPP with a limit of $2 million (building) and $1 million (business personal property), the Causes of Loss—Special Form, and the Replacement Cost optional coverage. While extinguishing a fire at the insured's location, firefighters disturbed stored chemicals that then leached into the soil. The cost to remove the soil and remediate the site was $45,000, and this expense was reported to the insurer within forty-five days of its occurrence. Determine whether any of the Additional Coverages of this policy apply to this loss. (Ignore the application of a deductible.)

Educational Objective 4

Determine whether the cause of a described loss is a covered cause of loss under either the Causes of Loss—Basic Form or the Causes of Loss—Broad Form.

Review Questions

4-1.   List the covered causes of loss in the Causes of Loss—Basic Form.

4-2.   Identify the causes of loss that are excluded under the Causes of Loss—Basic Form.

4-3. Identify the causes of loss that are covered under the Broad Form that are not covered under the Basic Form.

Application Question

4-4. The Murphy Corporation has a commercial property policy with a Causes of Loss—Basic Form covering its building. Explain whether each of the following losses would be covered under Murphy's policy. For those that would not be covered, identify a causes of loss form, if any, that would cover the loss.

a. A windstorm damaged Murphy's roof.

b. During a major storm, the river that runs near Murphy's property overflowed its banks. The rising water seeped into Murphy's building, damaging the hardwood floors.

c. Vandals broke several windows in Murphy's building.

    d.   Heavy earthquake shocks caused structural damage to Murphy's building.

Educational Objective 5

Determine whether the cause of a described loss is a Covered Cause of Loss under the Causes of Loss—Special Form.

Review Questions

5-1.   Identify the advantages to the insured of purchasing the Causes of Loss—Special Form.

5-2.   Identify examples of perils that the Special Form specifically excludes.

5-3.   Identify the purpose of the Loss or Damage to Products exclusion.

5-4. Identify examples of theft-related acts for which coverage is excluded under the Special Form.

5-5. Describe the characteristics of property that qualifies as Property in Transit under the BPP.

Application Question

5-6. Coverage for Jones's building and business personal property is currently subject to a Causes of Loss—Broad Form. When Jones renews his property insurance, he will purchase coverage subject to a Causes of Loss—Special Form, rather than a Broad Form. Briefly explain how the coverage for Jones's building and business personal property will be affected by this change in the causes of loss form.

Educational Objective 6

Apply the Limits of Insurance and Deductible provisions of the Building and Personal Property Coverage Form to a described loss.

Review Questions

6-1. Explain why the amount the insurer pays for a loss covered under the Building and Personal Property Coverage Form, also referred to as the BPP, is generally less than the applicable amount of insurance.

6-2. Contrast specific and blanket limits of insurance.

6-3. Explain how the BPP's deductible is applied following a loss, if the loss exceeds the deductible shown in the policy declarations.

6-4. Explain how the BPP's deductible is applied when the occurrence involves loss to more than one item of Covered Property and when separate limits of insurance apply.

6-5. What is the standard deductible for the BPP?

6-6. Explain why underwriters tend to prefer higher deductibles.

Application Question

6-7. Carl owns a souvenir store in Roswell, New Mexico. He insures his store under a BPP with a $400,000 building limit and a $1,000 deductible. Calculate how the policy would pay for losses valued at each of these amounts:

a. $800

b. $25,000

c. $415,000

Answers to Assignment 1 Questions

NOTE: These answers are provided to give students a basic understanding of acceptable types of responses. They often are not the only valid answers and are not intended to provide an exhaustive response to the questions.

Educational Objective 1

1-1. These are the components of a commercial property loss exposure:

- The type(s) of property
- The cause(s) of loss to property
- The financial consequences of property losses

1-2. Real property is tangible property consisting of land, all structures permanently attached to the land, and whatever is growing on the land. All property that is not real property is personal property.

1-3. For insurance purposes, personal property falls into these classifications:

- Contents
- Property in transit
- Property in the possession of others
- "Floating" property

1-4. A cause of loss adversely affects property and leaves it in an altered state. Some causes of loss do not alter the property (such as stolen property) but affect the owner's ability to use it.

1-5. The adverse financial consequences of a property loss may include a reduction in the value of the property, lost income, and/or extra expenses.

1-6. There are five components of a commercial property coverage part:

- Commercial property declarations
- One or more commercial property coverage forms
- One or more causes of loss forms
- Commercial Property Conditions
- Any applicable endorsements

1-7. A commercial property declarations page contains this property-specific information:

- A description of the property insured

- The kinds and amounts of coverage provided and the covered causes of loss (basic, broad, or special)

- A list of mortgagees, if any

- The deductible amount

- A list of the property coverage forms and endorsements attached to the policy

- The applicable coinsurance percentage(s)

- Any optional coverages

1-8. A commercial property coverage form typically contains these elements:

- Insuring agreement

- Delineation of the property covered and not covered

- Additional coverages and coverage extensions

- Provisions and definitions that apply only to that coverage form

1-9. The three types of causes of loss forms are basic, broad, and special.

Educational Objective 2

2-1. The three broad categories of property covered by the BPP are these:

- Building

- Your Business Personal Property

- Personal Property of Others

2-2. The BPP's definition of Building includes these elements:

- Buildings or structures listed and described in the declarations

- Completed additions to covered buildings

- Fixtures (including outdoor fixtures)

- Permanently installed machinery and equipment

- Personal property owned by the insured and used to maintain or service the building or its premises

- If they are not otherwise insured, additions, alterations, or repairs in progress

2-3. Except for an extension that provides limited coverage for property while away from the insured premises, coverage for Your Business Personal Property applies only when the property is located in or on the described Building or in the open (or in a vehicle) within 100 feet of the building or structure or within 100 feet of the described premises, whichever distance is greater.

2-4. Ignoring improvements and betterments when setting the amount of insurance a tenant should carry can result in severe underinsurance difficulties when a loss occurs.

2-5. Coverage for Personal Property of Others is designed to protect the insured against loss of or damage to the personal property of others while such property is in the custody of the insured. It is an important coverage for businesses (bailees) that have customers' property in their custody.

2-6. These are reasons for excluding some kinds of property from coverage:

- Some kinds of property, such as smuggled goods being held for sale, are illegal to insure.

- Some property may be much less susceptible to loss by most of the perils insured against.

- Some kinds of property are excluded because they can be insured more advantageously under other forms.

2-7. Because the EDP equipment policy specifically describes the computer hardware, its coverage is primary and will cover the loss for its $200,000 limit. The company's BPP policy will then cover the remaining $100,000 of the loss as business personal property.

Educational Objective 3

3-1. The limits for many of the BPP's additional coverages and coverage extensions can be increased by showing a higher limit in the declarations, adding an appropriate coverage endorsement, or buying another type of policy to supplement the BPP.

3-2. The BPP's Debris Removal additional coverage covers the cost of removing debris of covered property resulting from a covered cause of loss during the policy period. In some cases, the cost to remove debris of property that is not covered property is also covered.

3-3. The Preservation of Property additional coverage extends the policy to protect covered property while it is being moved and for up to thirty days at the new location.

3-4. The Pollutant Cleanup and Removal additional coverage provides limited coverage for the cleanup and removal of pollutants from land or water at the described premises.

3-5. The BPP excludes electronic data in most instances except as provided by the Electronic Data additional coverage because businesses are becoming increasingly reliant on electronic data and many insurers believe that the exposure is better treated by other forms of insurance.

3-6. Limited coverage for this loss would be provided by The Pollutant Cleanup and Removal additional coverage (in addition to the policy limit) for the "seepage" of pollutants caused by or resulting from a Covered Cause of Loss.

Educational Objective 4

4-1. The covered causes of loss in the Causes of Loss—Basic Form are fire, lightning, explosion, windstorm or hail, smoke, aircraft or vehicles, riot or civil commotion, vandalism, sprinkler leakage, sinkhole collapse, and volcanic action. Additional limited coverage is available for "fungus," wet rot, dry rot, and bacteria.

4-2. The causes of loss excluded from the Causes of Loss—Basic Form are ordinance or law; earth movement; governmental action; nuclear hazard; utility services; war and military action; water; "fungus," wet rot, dry rot, and bacteria; electrical, magnetic, or electromagnetic energy; rupturing or bursting of water pipes; leakage of water or steam; explosion of steam boilers, steam pipes, steam turbines, or steam engines; mechanical breakdown; and loss resulting from the neglect of the insured to use all reasonable means to save and preserve property at and after the time of loss.

4-3. The causes of loss covered under the Broad Form that are not covered under the Basic Form include these:

- Falling objects

- Weight of ice, snow, or sleet

- Water damage

4-4. A commercial property policy with a Causes of Loss—Basic Form provides this coverage:

a. Windstorm damage would be covered because windstorm is a covered peril under the Basic Form.

b. Damage from rising water would not be covered because of the flood exclusion. Flood is not a covered peril under any of the causes of loss forms. (Murphy needs to purchase coverage through the National Flood Insurance Program or by endorsement to its commercial property policy.)

c. Broken windows would be covered because vandalism is a covered cause of loss. (Although the vandalism peril once excluded glass breakage, that exclusion was eliminated in the 2000 revision.)

d. The structural damage would not be covered because of the earthquake exclusion. Murphy needs one of the earthquake endorsements.

Educational Objective 5

5-1. The Special Form offers these advantages to the insured:

- Certain causes of loss that are omitted or excluded under the Broad Form are not excluded—and are therefore covered—under the Special Form.

- By covering direct physical losses other than those that are specifically excluded, the Special Form covers losses that the insured might not have anticipated.

- The Special Form shifts the burden of proof from the insured to the insurer.

5-2. Examples of perils that the Special Form specifically excludes are these:

- Wear and tear

- Rust, corrosion, decay, deterioration, or hidden or latent defect

- Smog

- Settling, cracking, shrinking, or expansion

- Infestations and waste products of insects, birds, rodents, or other animals

- Mechanical breakdown

- Dampness or dryness of atmosphere, changes or extremes in temperatures, or marring or scratching (applicable to personal property only)

5-3. The Loss or Damage to Products exclusion eliminates coverage for damage to merchandise, goods, or other products resulting from production errors, such as adding wrong ingredients or measuring ingredients incorrectly.

5-4. Examples of theft-related acts for which coverage is excluded under the Special Form include these:

- Dishonest or criminal acts (including theft) of the insured or of partners, members, officers, managers, directors, or employees of the insured

- The voluntary surrendering of property as the result of a fraudulent scheme or trickery

- Loss by theft of construction materials not attached as part of the building

- Loss of property that is simply missing without explanation or that is evidenced only by an inventory shortage

5-5. To qualify as Property in Transit under the BPP, property must be in or on a motor vehicle owned, leased, or operated by the insured and cannot be in the custody of the insured's sales personnel.

5-6. With the Special Form, Jones's building and business personal property form will have coverage for accidental and unforeseen risks of direct physical loss subject to exclusions and limitations expressed in the form. With the Broad Form, Jones's building and business personal property form had coverage for the listed perils.

Educational Objective 6

6-1. The amount that the insurer pays for a loss covered under the Building and Personal Property Coverage Form, also referred to as the BPP, is generally less than the applicable amount of insurance because total commercial property losses are rare, and the BPP contains limitations in addition to the limit of insurance that reduce the amount the insurer pays.

6-2. When specific limits are used, the declarations show separate limits of insurance for each covered building and for personal property at each location. A blanket limit can apply one amount of insurance to all property covered by the policy.

6-3. If a loss exceeds the deductible shown in the policy declarations, the deductible is subtracted from the loss, not from the limit of the insurance.

6-4. When the occurrence involves loss to more than one item of Covered Property and when separate limits of insurance apply, the losses will not be combined in determining application of the deductible. But the deductible will be applied only once per occurrence.

6-5. Under the Insurance Services Office, Inc. (ISO) *Commercial Lines Manual* (CLM) rules, the standard BPP deductible is $500.

6-6. Underwriters tend to prefer higher deductibles because they save the insurer the expense of handling small claims.

6-7. Carl's BPP with a $400,000 building limit and a $1,000 deductible would pay these amounts for losses:

   a. $800—BPP pays nothing.

   b. $25,000—BPP pays $24,000.

   c. $415,000—BPP pays $400,000.

Direct Your Learning ▶▶

Commercial Property Insurance, Part II

Educational Objectives

After learning the content of this assignment, you should be able to:

1. Explain how each of the Loss Conditions and Additional Conditions affects coverage under the Building and Personal Property Coverage Form.

2. Explain how each of the following optional coverages described in the BPP modifies the basic coverage of the BPP:

    - Agreed Value

    - Inflation Guard

    - Replacement Cost

    - Extension of Replacement Cost to Personal Property of Others

3. Summarize each of the Commercial Property Conditions.

4. Explain how each of the conditions contained in the Common Policy Conditions affects coverage under a commercial property coverage part.

5. Explain how each of these documents modifies the Building and Personal Property Coverage Form:

    - Ordinance or Law Coverage endorsement

    - Spoilage Coverage endorsement

    - Flood Coverage endorsement

    - Earthquake and Volcanic Eruption Coverage endorsement

    - Peak Season Limit of Insurance endorsement

    - Value Reporting Form

2

6. Identify the factors that affect commercial property insurance premiums.

7. Given a case, determine whether, and for what amount, a described loss would be covered by a commercial property coverage part that includes the Building and Personal Property Coverage Form and any of the three causes of loss forms.

Outline

▸ **BPP Loss Conditions and Additional Conditions**
  A. Abandonment
  B. Appraisal
  C. Duties in the Event of Loss or Damage
  D. Loss Payment
  E. Recovered Property
  F. Vacancy
  G. Valuation
  H. Coinsurance
  I. Mortgageholder

▸ **BPP: Optional Coverages**
  A. Agreed Value
  B. Inflation Guard
  C. Replacement Cost
  D. Extension of Replacement Cost to Personal Property of Others

▸ **Commercial Property Conditions**
  A. Concealment, Misrepresentation, or Fraud
  B. Control of Property
  C. Insurance Under Two or More Coverages
  D. Legal Action Against Us
  E. Liberalization
  F. Transfer of Rights of Recovery Against Others to Us
  G. No Benefit to Bailee
  H. Other Insurance
  I. Policy Period, Coverage Territory

▸ **Common Policy Conditions**
  A. Cancellation
  B. Changes
  C. Examination of Books and Records
  D. Inspections and Surveys
  E. Premiums
  F. Transfer of Rights and Duties Under This Policy

▸ **Commercial Property Endorsements**
  A. Ordinance or Law Coverage
  B. Spoilage Coverage
  C. Flood Coverage
  D. Earthquake and Volcanic Eruption Coverage
  E. Peak Season Limit of Insurance Endorsement
  F. Value Reporting Form

▸ **Factors Affecting Commercial Property Premiums**
  A. Rating Fundamentals
  B. Aspects of Coverage Affecting Premiums
    1. Limit of Insurance
    2. Covered Causes of Loss
    3. Coinsurance Percentage
    4. Deductible Amount
    5. Optional Coverages
  C. Other Factors Affecting Premiums
    1. Construction
    2. Occupancy
    3. Protection
    4. External Exposure
    5. Location

▸ **Determining Whether the BPP Covers a Loss**
  A. Case Facts
  B. Necessary Reference Materials
  C. Overview of Steps
  D. Determination of Coverage
    1. DICE Analysis Step 1: Declarations
    2. DICE Analysis Step 2: Insuring Agreement
    3. DICE Analysis Step 3: Conditions
    4. DICE Analysis Step 4: Exclusions
  E. Determination of Amount Payable

s.m.a.r.t. tips Reduce the number of Key Words and Phrases that you must review. SMART Flash Cards contain the Key Words and Phrases and their definitions, allowing you to set aside those cards that you have mastered.

For each assignment, you should define or describe each of the Key Words and Phrases and answer each of the Review and Application Questions.

Educational Objective 1

Explain how each of the Loss Conditions and Additional Conditions affects coverage under the Building and Personal Property Coverage Form.

Key Words and Phrases

Proof of loss

Actual cash value (ACV)

Review Questions

1-1. According to the BPP's Abandonment condition, who is responsible for making arrangements for the repair or disposal of covered property?

1-2. What does the BPP specify as the insured's duties in the event of a loss?

1-3. Describe the insurer's options in loss payment as established in the BPP.

1-4. Describe the rights granted to a mortgage holder that is named on the declarations page of a commercial property policy.

Application Question

1-5. An office building with an actual cash value (ACV) of $300,000 is covered under a BPP, subject to an 80 percent coinsurance provision.

    a.   What is the minimum amount of insurance that must be purchased on this building on an ACV basis to avoid a coinsurance penalty?

    b.   Assume that the owner purchased $180,000 coverage (ACV) on the building. What amount would the owner be paid in the event of a $100,000 covered loss (ACV) to the building? Disregard any deductible that might apply.

Educational Objective 2

Explain how each of the following optional coverages described in the BPP modifies the basic coverage of the BPP:

- **Agreed Value**
- **Inflation Guard**
- **Replacement Cost**
- **Extension of Replacement Cost to Personal Property of Others**

Key Words and Phrases

Agreed Value optional coverage

Inflation Guard optional coverage

Replacement Cost optional coverage

Review Questions

2-1. List the four optional coverages available in the BPP.

2-2. Describe the purpose and operation of the Agreed Value optional coverage in the BPP.

2-3. When the insured chooses the Replacement Cost option under the BPP, how is the Coinsurance condition affected?

Application Question

2-4. Sadie owns a call center business in Rochester, New York, and insures her building and personal property under a BPP. Because communications technology changes so rapidly, she leases all of her phone equipment. According to the lease agreement, she is responsible for the replacement cost of the leased phone equipment in the event it is damaged. What should Sadie do to ensure that she has insurance coverage sufficient to meet the obligations of her lease agreement?

Educational Objective 3
Summarize each of the Commercial Property Conditions.

Key Word or Phrase

Subrogation

Review Questions

3-1. Contrast misrepresentation and concealment.

3-2. Summarize the two parts of the BPP's Control of Property condition.

3-3. Describe the two requirements an insured must meet before legal action can be brought against an insurer to enforce a commercial property policy.

3-4. Describe the BPP's Liberalization condition.

Educational Objective 4

Explain how each of the conditions contained in the Common Policy Conditions affects coverage under a commercial property coverage part.

Review Questions

4-1. Describe how a policy may be canceled by an insurer or an insured according to the Common Policy Conditions.

4-2. According to the Common Policy Conditions, over what time period is the insurer permitted to examine and audit the insured's books and records related to the policy?

4-3. According to the Common Policy Conditions, under what circumstances can the insured transfer rights or duties under a policy?

Educational Objective 5

Explain how each of these documents modifies the Building and Personal Property Coverage Form:

- Ordinance or Law Coverage endorsement
- Spoilage Coverage endorsement
- Flood Coverage endorsement
- Earthquake and Volcanic Eruption Coverage endorsement
- Peak Season Limit of Insurance endorsement
- Value Reporting Form

Review Questions

5-1.   Identify examples of tasks for which the BPP's endorsements are useful.

5-2.   Under the Spoilage Coverage endorsement, what must cause the spoilage of perishable stock in order for the spoilage to be covered?

5-3.   Identify the two sources of flood insurance for buildings and their contents.

5-4. Contrast the two Insurance Services Office, Inc. (ISO) earthquake and volcanic eruption endorsements.

5-5. Explain how the Peak Season Limit of Insurance endorsement covers the fluctuating values of business personal property.

5-6. Explain how the Value Reporting Form covers the fluctuating values of business personal property.

5-7. Explain why many insurers would decline to issue a Value Reporting Form for a smaller insured.

Educational Objective 6
Identify the factors that affect commercial property insurance premiums.

Key Word or Phrase

External exposure

Review Questions

6-1. Define rating.

6-2. What is class rating?

6-3. How is specific rating different from class rating?

6-4. Explain why the limit of insurance applicable to the coverage is an important component of the final premium.

6-5. Identify the components of the rate for the Causes of Loss—Basic Form.

6-6. Identify the coinsurance-related assumption under which the rates ordinarily used for insuring buildings and personal property are calculated.

6-7. Identify the deductible-related assumption under which the rates ordinarily used for insuring buildings and personal property are calculated.

Application Question

6-8. Etchley Clothing owns a red brick building that it occupies as a retail clothing store. Etchley is purchasing a commercial property policy from Radley Insurance Company with a Causes of Loss—Broad Form for this building. Etchley has selected a policy with a limit of $500,000 on the building on a replacement cost basis with a 90 percent coinsurance clause and a $1,000 deductible. Because Etchley's building is located fifteen miles from the nearest fire department and twenty miles from a police station, it has installed a sprinkler system and a burglar alarm.

a. In rating Etchley's commercial property policy, what factors will Radley consider?

b. How will the factors you identified affect the premium for this policy?

Educational Objective 7

Given a case, determine whether, and for what amount, a described loss would be covered by a commercial property coverage part that includes the Building and Personal Property Coverage Form and any of the three causes of loss forms.

Application Question

7-1. A two-story antique store owned by Chris was damaged by fire. The building is a restored Victorian mansion insured on an actual cash value (ACV) basis under the Building and Personal Property Coverage Form. The features of the building include original hardwood floors, hand-carved woodwork, and a slate roof. The limit of insurance is $280,000. The policy has an 80 percent coinsurance requirement and a $1,000 deductible that applies to all covered losses. The fire caused $72,000 in damages (ACV) to Chris's building. At the time of the fire, the building had an ACV of $400,000, a market value of $500,000, and a functional replacement cost of $250,000.

    a.   Calculate the dollar amount Chris will be paid for this loss.

    b.   How would the Functional Building Valuation Endorsement affect the calculation of the dollar amount that Chris would receive for the loss?

Answers to Assignment 2 Questions

NOTE: These answers are provided to give students a basic understanding of acceptable types of responses. They often are not the only valid answers and are not intended to provide an exhaustive response to the questions.

Educational Objective 1

1-1. The Abandonment condition clarifies that making arrangements for the repair or disposal of covered property is the insured's responsibility, unless the insurer chooses to exercise its option under the Loss Payment condition.

1-2. The insured's duties in the event of loss include these:

- Notify the police if the loss appears to have resulted from a violation of law, such as vandalism, arson, or theft.

- Give the insurer prompt notice of the loss, including a description of the property damaged. Prompt notice is generally held to mean as soon as feasible under the circumstances.

- Provide information as to how, when, and where the loss occurred.

- Take all reasonable steps to protect the property from further loss.

- At the insurer's request, furnish the insurer with inventories of the damaged and undamaged property and permit the insurer to inspect the property and records.

- Submit to examination under oath regarding any matter related to the loss.

- Cooperate with the insurer in the adjustment of the loss.

- Send a signed, sworn proof of loss to the insurer within sixty days after the insurer's request for one.

1-3. The insurer's options in loss payment as established in the BPP include these:

- Pay the amount of loss or damage.

- Pay the cost of repairing or replacing the damaged property.

- Take over all or any part of the property and pay its agreed or appraised value.

- Repair, rebuild, or replace the damaged property with other property of like kind and quality.

1-4. A mortgage holder named on the declarations page of a commercial property policy would have these rights:

- Payment for any claim for loss on the covered mortgaged property

- Notification of cancellation or nonrenewal

1-5. These answers address questions regarding actual cash value:

a. The minimum amount of insurance that must be purchased on an ACV basis to avoid a coinsurance penalty is calculated as follows:

$0.80 \times \$300,000 = \$240,000$

b. The amount the owner would be paid in the event of a $100,000 covered loss (ACV) is as follows:

$180,000/$240,000 × $100,000 = $75,000

Educational Objective 2

2-1. The four optional coverages available in the BPP are as follows:

- Agreed Value

- Inflation Guard

- Replacement Cost

- Extension of Replacement Cost to Personal Property of Others

2-2. The purpose of the Agreed Value optional coverage in the BPP is to remove the uncertainty as to whether the amount of insurance carried complies with the Coinsurance condition. The option suspends the Coinsurance condition if the insured carries the amount of insurance that the insurer and insured agree to be the property's full value.

2-3. When the insured chooses the Replacement Cost option under the BPP, the Coinsurance condition continues to apply, but the amount of insurance required by the Coinsurance condition is calculated by multiplying replacement cost by the coinsurance percentage if the claim is made on a replacement cost basis.

2-4. Sadie should select the Replacement Cost optional coverage, and she should further elect to have the personal property of others valued at replacement cost. In that way, the amount of the loss to the leased phone equipment is calculated according to the terms of the lease (but the amount of loss cannot exceed the replacement cost of the property or the applicable limit of insurance).

Educational Objective 3

3-1. Misrepresentation is an active, deliberate misstatement of fact. Concealment, in contrast, is an intentional failure to disclose a material fact.

3-2. The first part of the Control of Property condition states that coverage under the policy will not be affected by acts or omissions of persons other than the insured if those persons are not acting under the direction or control of the insured. The second part of the condition states that violation of a policy condition at one location will not affect coverage at another location.

3-3. The two requirements an insured must meet before legal action can be brought against an insurer to enforce a commercial property policy are these:

a. The insured must comply with all conditions of the policy, including those in the coverage part and the common policy conditions, as well as the applicable loss conditions.

b. The action must be brought within two years after the date on which the direct physical loss occurred.

3-4. Under the BPP's Liberalization condition, if the insurer adopts any revision that would broaden coverage under the commercial property coverage part and for which there is no additional premium charge, the broader coverage is extended automatically to policies already in effect.

Educational Objective 4

4-1. According to the Common Policy Conditions, an insurer can cancel a policy by mailing or delivering written notice of cancellation to the first named insured at least ten days before the cancellation date if cancellation is for nonpayment of premium, or thirty days for any other reason. The insured may cancel a policy anytime by mailing or delivering written notice of cancellation.

4-2. According to the Common Policy Conditions, the insurer is permitted to examine and audit the insured's books and records at any time during the policy period and for up to three years after the policy's termination.

4-3. According to the Common Policy Conditions, the insured must have the insurer's written consent to transfer rights or duties under a policy. However, if an individual named insured dies, the coverage automatically transfers to the insured's legal representative or the person having proper temporary custody of the insured property.

Educational Objective 5

5-1. The BPP's endorsements are useful for providing coverage enhancements that some insureds may want but that others either do not believe they need or cannot afford, eliminating coverage for certain exposures, enabling underwriters to accept applications that they would otherwise decline, changing policy provisions to match the specific characteristics of certain industries or insureds, and amending the policy to comply with state insurance regulations.

5-2. The Spoilage Coverage endorsement covers spoilage resulting from a power outage or an on-premises breakdown or contamination of the insured's refrigerating, cooling, or humidity control equipment.

5-3. The two sources of flood insurance for buildings and their contents are the National Flood Insurance Program (NFIP) and private insurers without federal participation.

5-4. The main difference between the two earthquake and volcanic eruption endorsements is that one is written for the full policy limit and contains a coinsurance requirement, whereas the other is written subject to a sublimit that is lower than the regular policy limit and does not contain a coinsurance requirement.

5-5. The Peak Season Limit of Insurance endorsement covers the fluctuating values of business personal property by providing differing amounts of insurance for certain time frames during the policy period.

5-6. The Value Reporting Form covers the fluctuating values of business personal property by providing insurance for the insured's maximum expected values and requiring the insured to periodically report property values to the insurer. The insurer calculates the final policy premium based on the reported values instead of the limit of insurance.

5-7. Many insurers would decline to issue a Value Reporting Form for a smaller insured because the premium may not be large enough to warrant the added expense of processing the reports and calculating the final premium.

Educational Objective 6

6-1. Rating is the process of applying a rate to a particular exposure and performing any other necessary calculations to determine an appropriate policy premium.

6-2. Class rating is a rating approach that uses rates reflecting the average probability of loss for businesses within large groups of similar risks.

6-3. Specific rating develops rates that reflect the exposure to loss of a particular business. Class rating develops rates that reflect the average probability of loss for businesses within a large group of similar risks by generalizing about the probabilities of loss within these groups.

6-4. The limit of insurance applicable to the coverage is an important component of the final premium because it represents the exposure against which the applicable rate is multiplied to calculate the premium.

6-5. The rate for the Causes of Loss—Basic Form consists of a Group I rate (for fire, lightning, explosion, vandalism, and sprinkler leakage) and a Group II rate (for all other causes of loss covered under the Basic Form).

6-6. The rates ordinarily used for insuring buildings and personal property are calculated with the assumption that they will be used with an 80 percent coinsurance clause in the policy. These rates are therefore called the "80 percent coinsurance rates."

6-7. Commercial property rates are developed with the assumption that the policy will be subject to a $500 deductible.

6-8. These answers are based on the Etchley Corporation and Radley Insurance Company case.

   a. Radley will consider these factors:

   - Construction (brick)

   - Occupancy (retail clothing store)

   - Causes-of-loss form (broad)

   - Building limit ($500,000)

   - Coinsurance (90%)

   - Deductible ($1,000)

   - Location (territory)

   - Fire protection (fifteen miles from fire station, sprinkler system)

    b.   These factors will affect the premium as specified:

- The brick (masonry) construction will carry a lower rate than a frame building but a higher one than a fire-resistive building.

- Occupancies are rated according to how risky they are. The occupancy (retail clothing store) would probably not be considered particularly hazardous and would carry an average rate.

- The Causes of Loss—Broad Form would have a higher premium than a Basic Form but a lower premium than a Special Form.

- The building limit is used to determine the exposure unit to be multiplied by the rate to determine the premium. (Property rates are usually per $100 of insurance, so in this case: 5,000 × rate = premium.)

- Etchley's premium would be reduced because its coinsurance percentage is higher than 80 percent and its deductible is higher than the base deductible.

- Although a high rate would apply because the building is many miles from the nearest fire station, a credit would probably be given for the sprinkler system.

- NOTE: The burglar alarm and the distance from the police station would probably not be considered in this case. Property rates are generally based on fire protection; also, since the Broad Form does not include theft coverage, crime protection is not a valid factor.

    The replacement cost option does not affect the rate (but it does affect the amount of insurance Etchley needs to satisfy the coinsurance requirement).

Educational Objective 7

7-1. These answers apply to the antique store case:

    a.   The dollar amount Chris will be paid for this loss is calculated as shown:

$0.80 \times \$400{,}000 = \$320{,}000$

$(\$280{,}000/\$320{,}000 \times \$72{,}000) - \$1{,}000 = \$62{,}000$

    b.   For functional replacement, the loss would be limited to the smallest of the limit of insurance, the market value of the building, or the functional replacement cost. The lowest of these limits is $250,000. The deductible would apply, but coinsurance does not apply. Therefore, the amount payable would be calculated as $72,000 – $1,000 (deductible) = $71,000.

Direct Your Learning ▶▶

Business Income Insurance

Educational Objectives

After learning the content of this assignment, you should be able to:

1. Describe the following aspects of the business income loss exposure:

   - Measurement of business income loss

   - Effect of business interruption on expenses

   - Property and perils involved in business income losses

2. Summarize the provisions of the Business Income and Extra Expense insuring agreements in the ISO business income coverage (BIC) forms.

3. Explain how each of the additional coverages and the coverage extension supplement the business income coverage (BIC) forms.

4. Summarize the Limits of Insurance, Loss Conditions, and Additional Condition (Coinsurance) of the business income coverage (BIC) forms.

5. Explain how the optional coverages each modify the business income coverage (BIC) forms.

6. Given a case, determine whether, and for what amount, a described loss would be covered either by the Business Income (and Extra Expense) Coverage Form or the Business Income (Without Extra Expense) Coverage Form.

Outline

▶ **Business Income Loss Exposures**

A. Measurement of Business Income Losses

B. Effect of Business Interruption on Expenses

   1. Continuing Expenses

   2. Extra Expenses

C. Property and Perils Involved in Business Income Losses

▶ **BIC Insuring Agreements**

A. Business Income Insuring Agreement

B. Extra Expense Insuring Agreement

▶ **BIC Additional Coverages and Coverage Extension**

A. Expenses to Reduce Loss

B. Civil Authority

C. Alterations and New Buildings

D. Extended Business Income

E. Interruption of Computer Operations

F. Newly Acquired Locations

▶ **BIC Limit of Insurance and Conditions**

A. Limits of Insurance

B. Loss Conditions

   1. Appraisal

   2. Duties in the Event of Loss

   3. Loss Determination

   4. Loss Payment

C. Additional Condition: Coinsurance

▶ **BIC Optional Coverages**

A. Maximum Period of Indemnity

B. Monthly Limit of Indemnity

C. Business Income Agreed Value

D. Extended Period of Indemnity

▶ **Determining Whether the BIC Form Covers a Loss**

A. Case Facts

B. Necessary Reference Materials

C. Determination of Coverage

   1. DICE Analysis Step 1: Declarations

   2. DICE Analysis Step 2: Insuring Agreement

   3. DICE Analysis Step 3: Conditions

   4. DICE Analysis Step 4: Exclusions

D. Determination of Amounts Payable

Actively capture information by using the open space in the SMART Review Notes to write out key concepts. Putting information into your own words is an effective way to push that information into your memory.

For each assignment, you should define or describe each of the Key Words and Phrases and answer each of the Review and Application Questions.

Educational Objective 1

Describe the following aspects of the business income loss exposure:

- **Measurement of business income loss**
- **Effect of business interruption on expenses**
- **Property and perils involved in business income losses**

Key Words and Phrases

Business income insurance

Net income

Profit

Net loss

Continuing expenses

Noncontinuing expenses

Extra expenses

Review Questions

1-1.   How can business income losses be measured?

1-2.   Give three examples of normal operating expenses that could continue during a short business interruption.

1-3.   Give three examples of extra expenses that might be incurred to continue operations after a physical loss.

1-4.   In order for business income insurance to apply, what must occur, according to the usual business income insuring agreement?

Application Question

1-5. Surewell Aircraft manufactures small single-engine aircraft. It annually assembles 100 aircraft at its plant in Arizona from composite-material bodies manufactured in Mexico and engines manufactured in England specifically for Surewell's aircraft. Analyze Surewell's business income loss exposures.

Educational Objective 2

Summarize the provisions of the Business Income and Extra Expense insuring agreements in the ISO business income coverage (BIC) forms.

Review Questions

2-1. Describe the application of the following terms found in the Business Income insuring agreement, as indicated in the following context:

a. What must the "suspension" result from?

b. What are the "operations" in relation to business activities of the insured and rental value coverage?

    c.   When does the "period of restoration" begin and end?

2-2. Explain how extra expenses to repair or replace property are treated differently than other extra expenses in the Extra Expense insuring agreement.

2-3. Explain how the definition of premises is broadened if the insured is a tenant.

Application Questions

2-4. Anton and Lynne decided to sell yoga merchandise in a small room of their yoga studio. A month after they purchased insurance, several of the studio's windows were broken as the result of a windstorm, which also ruined most of their merchandise. In an attempt to fill customer orders, Anton and Lynne paid $2,000 in overnight shipping costs to replace the damaged goods. Had they not paid for expedited shipping, they would have lost $3,000 in merchandise sales. Explain whether their Business Income (Without Extra Expense) Coverage Form will pay for the overnight shipping cost.

2-5. Jack's auto repair shop is covered under a business income coverage (BIC) form. His shop incurs a covered business income loss. It will take two months to reopen his shop. The net profit he would have earned during that time is $10,000. His continuing operating expenses of rent, taxes, and insurance (but no salary) total $4,000 for two months. Explain what will be considered part of Jack's business income loss.

Educational Objective 3

Explain how each of the additional coverages and the coverage extension supplement the business income coverage (BIC) forms.

Review Questions

3-1. Explain a danger to an insured covered by the Business Income (Without Extra Expense) Coverage Form regarding expenses incurred to reduce loss.

3-2. Explain the purpose of Alterations and New Buildings additional coverage in the business income coverage (BIC) forms.

3-3. Explain the purpose of Interruption of Computer Operations additional coverage in the BIC.

Application Questions

3-4. Janet is a dentist whose dental office was damaged in a windstorm, which is a covered cause of loss. She is insured under a BIC without extra expense form. The period of restoration lasted seven months, but her office is now restored. Unfortunately, not all of her patients have returned. Will her BIC policy provide coverage? Please explain your answer.

3-5. Bob repairs computer equipment in his shop. His business has been rapidly expanding, and sixty days ago, he opened a new store. This new store recently had a fire loss involving extensive property damage, which made the store unusable. He is insured under a BIC and paid additional premium for the Newly Acquired Locations coverage extension. Bob did not report the existence of his new store to his insurer until the day of the fire. Will this coverage extension respond to Bob's fire loss? Please explain your answer.

Educational Objective 4

Summarize the Limits of Insurance, Loss Conditions, and Additional Condition (Coinsurance) of the business income coverage (BIC) forms.

Key Word or Phrase

Probable maximum loss (PML)

Review Questions

4-1. Compare writing the limits of insurance for business income on a specific basis with doing so on a blanket basis.

4-2. Describe how the amount of a business income loss is determined in the BIC.

4-3. What are the different coinsurance percentages that can be used with the BIC?

4-4. How is the denominator of the business income coinsurance formula calculated?

Application Question

4-5. Susan's Sporting Goods is insured for $60,000 under a business income coverage form that contains a 50 percent coinsurance clause. After a fire, Susan was forced to close her store for one month before she could reopen for business. If the fire had not occurred, Susan's net income and operating expenses at the store for the twelve months following the policy inception date would have been $180,000. For the month that the store was closed, Susan's business income loss (net income lost plus continuing operating expenses) was $12,000. What dollar amount will Susan recover from her insurer for this business income loss? (Hint: Don't overlook the coinsurance clause.) Show your calculations.

Educational Objective 5

Explain how the optional coverages each modify the business income coverage (BIC) forms.

Review Questions

5-1. Identify the three optional business income coverages that eliminate or suspend the Coinsurance condition.

5-2. When is the only time insureds should add the Maximum Period of Indemnity coverage option to their business income insurance?

5-3. Describe the two steps necessary to activate the Business Income Agreed Value coverage option.

5-4. Why is the Extended Period of Indemnity coverage option so attractive to insureds that own restaurants and clothing stores?

Application Questions

5-5. Brad is an insured who purchased business income coverage. He chose the Maximum Period of Indemnity optional coverage to suspend any Coinsurance penalty. Describe how covered losses will be calculated in the following scenarios:

a. Brad's policy limit is $60,000. His business income loss is $50,000 per month for a period of restoration that lasted 90 days, or three months after the three-day deductible.

b. Brad's policy limit is $600,000. His business income loss is $50,000 per month for a period of restoration that lasted 180 days, or six months after the three-day deductible.

5-6. Sally owns a restaurant and purchased business income insurance with a limit of $500,000 and the Extended Period of Indemnity (EPI) optional coverage. The EPI optional coverage replaced the 60 days of the Extended Business Income (EBI) additional coverage with 90 days of EPI. Within the policy period, Sally's restaurant suffered a fire that caused a total suspension of operations resulting in $300,000 loss of business income during the period of restoration. After the restaurant was repaired and resumed its operations, it incurred additional reduction of its normal business income amounting to $40,000 per month for 180 consecutive days. Assuming that one month equals 30 consecutive days, and also assuming no coinsurance problems, what additional amount will Sally's insurer pay for the restaurant's loss of business income occurring after the restaurant resumed operations?

Educational Objective 6

Given a case, determine whether, and for what amount, a described loss would be covered either by the Business Income (and Extra Expense) Coverage Form or the Business Income (Without Extra Expense) Coverage Form.

Application Question

6-1. Mighty Fine Jewelry (MFJ) is a retail jewelry store. It owns and occupies one half of the building it operates its store in. The other half is owned by MFJ but is rented to a coffee shop. MFJ is insured under a commercial package policy that includes the Business Income (and Extra Expense) Coverage Form, the Causes of Loss—Special Form, the Commercial Property Conditions, and the Common Policy Conditions. The Commercial Property Coverage Part Declarations Page describes the insured premises at the address of the store building owned by MFJ and shows a $500,000 Business Income limit of insurance for the location, subject to option (2), Business Income Other Than "Rental Value." The one-year policy period shown in the declarations began on January 1, 20X1.

On December 1, 20X1, the coffee shop had an electrical fire that caused enough damage to close it for two months. MFJ also incurred damage from this covered loss when smoke spewed into MFJ's part of the building. Since the smoke damage occurred during the peak season before Christmas, MFJ quickly repaired the damage by painting the ceiling and walls as well as replacing the carpets and cleaning the display cabinets. MFJ was able to reopen for business within seventy-two hours after the fire.

MFJ lost $10,000 in rental income for the two months that the coffee shop was closed for repair. MFJ also lost $4,000 in business income while it was closed. MFJ and the insurer agreed on all loss determinations and that MFJ fulfilled all its post-loss duties under the policy. Coinsurance is not a consideration for the purposes of this case. The following questions concern the business income fire loss of MFJ:

a. Using the DICE method, Step 1: Declarations, does the declarations page support coverage for MFJ's loss of business income?

b. Using the DICE method, Step 2: Insuring Agreement, does the Business Income insuring agreement support coverage for MFJ's loss of business income?

Answers to Assignment 3 Questions

NOTE: These answers are provided to give students a basic understanding of acceptable types of responses. They often are not the only valid answers and are not intended to provide an exhaustive response to the questions.

Educational Objective 1

1-1. A business income loss can be measured as the reduction in the firm's net income (the difference between what the firm would have earned had no loss occurred and what the firm actually did earn during the period of interruption).

1-2. Three examples of normal operating expenses that could continue during a short interruption are payroll of key employees, debt repayments, and taxes.

1-3. Three examples of extra expenses are the cost to rent temporary office space, overtime wages to employees, and overnight air shipment of needed repair parts.

1-4. In order for business income insurance to apply, there must be an interruption of operations caused by property damage from a covered peril to property at locations or situations described in the policy, resulting in a loss of business income and/or extra expense.

1-5. Surewell's business income loss exposures include these:

- Loss of income from the manufacture and sales of the aircraft.

- Extra expenses to rent equipment and a facility while its plant is being restored.

- Two key suppliers provide aircraft bodies and engines. Damage to either of these plants could shut down Surewell's production and sales.

Educational Objective 2

2-1. The significance of "suspension," "operations," and "period of restoration" in the Business Income insuring agreement is this:

   a. The "suspension" must result from direct physical loss or damage to real or personal property caused by a covered cause of loss and occurring at the "premises" described in the declarations.

   b. The "operations" of the insured are (1) the business activities of the insured that occur at the premises described in the declarations or (2) in the case of rental value coverage, the "tenant-ability" (suitability for occupancy) of the described premises.

   c. The "period of restoration" begins seventy-two hours after the physical loss occurs and ends when the property is (or should have been) restored to use with reasonable speed.

2-2. Extra expenses to repair or replace property are covered only to the extent that they actually reduce the business income loss. Other extra expenses, such as the costs to move to a temporary location, increased rent at the temporary location, rental of substitute equipment (furniture, fixtures, or machinery), and the cost of substitute services such as data processing, are covered in full, subject to the policy limit, and are not limited to the amount by which they reduce the extra expense loss. Coverage applies even if the business income loss is not reduced at all.

2-3. If the insured is a tenant, the definition of premises is broadened to include "any area within the building or on the site…if that area services, or is used to gain access to, the described premises."

2-4. Under the Business Income (Without Extra Expense) Coverage Form, Anton and Lynne's insurer will pay the $2,000 in overnight shipping costs because doing so will reduce the $3,000 in business income loss that would have been incurred had they not paid for the expedited shipping. Conversely, if the cost to ship the merchandise did not reduce the business income loss, the Business Income (Without Extra Expense) coverage would not cover the expedited shipping.

2-5. The BIC defines business income as the sum of these two items:

- Net profit or loss that would have been earned or incurred if the suspension had not occurred. Subject to a seventy-two hour waiting period, Jack's loss of a net profit of $10,000 during those two months will be included in the definition.

- Normal operating expenses, including payroll, that continue during the suspension. Jack's continuing operating expenses, which are rent, taxes, and insurance totaling $4,000, will be included in the definition.

Educational Objective 3

3-1. An insured can incur the same types of expenses that are covered under the Business Income (and Extra Expense) Coverage Form, but they are covered only to the extent that they reduce business income loss. Thus, a danger of the business income without extra expense form is that the insured may incur extra expenses other than the reduction in business income loss. The result could be a large, uninsured extra expense loss.

3-2. The purpose of the Alterations and New Buildings additional coverage is to provide coverage for loss of income resulting from a delay in beginning operations if the delay results from damage at the described premises by a covered cause of loss to any of the following:

- New buildings or structures, either completed or under construction

- Alterations or additions to existing buildings

- Machinery, equipment, supplies, or building materials located on or within 100 feet of the described premises (provided they are used in the construction, alterations, or additions or are incidental to the occupancy of new buildings)

3-3. The purpose of the Interruption of Computer Operations additional coverage is to provide $2,500 of coverage for all loss of business income or extra expense when business operations are suspended due to an interruption of computer operations resulting from the destruction or corruption of electronic data caused by a covered cause of loss.

3-4. Janet's situation is not unique, and the Extended Business Income (EBI) additional coverage in her policy is designed to address this possibility. It does so by extending the regular business income coverage to include business income losses that continue after the period of restoration ends. Her coverage begins when the damaged property has been restored, which it has, and ends when her business returns to normal. This additional coverage is subject to a maximum of sixty days.

3-5. Bob's Newly Acquired Locations coverage extension probably would have covered this loss if he had reported the new store within thirty days of the date he opened it. Because it took him sixty days to report the existence of the new store to the insurer, the coverage extension will probably not apply.

Educational Objective 4

4-1. If the limits of insurance for business income are written on a specific basis, a specific limit is set for each building insured. If they are written on a blanket basis, the limit applies to all buildings at one location or to all buildings at multiple locations.

4-2. The amount of business income loss is determined on the basis of the following:

- The net income of the business before the loss occurred

- The probable net income of the business if no loss had occurred

- The operating expenses that must continue during the period of restoration to permit the insured to resume operations with the quality of service that existed prior to loss

- Other relevant sources of information

4-3. The coinsurance percentages that can be used with the BIC are 50, 60, 70, 80, 90, 100, 125, or no coinsurance.

4-4. The denominator of the BIC coinsurance formula is determined by multiplying the coinsurance percentage by the sum of the insured's net income (whether profit or loss) plus all operating expenses (less certain expenses) that would have been incurred in the absence of a loss for the twelve-month period beginning at the inception or latest anniversary date of the policy.

4-5. Susan's Sporting Goods will recover the following from her insurer for the business income loss resulting from the fire:

The coinsurance formula is:

Loss payment equals the amount of insurance carried divided by the amount of insurance required multiplied by the loss amount.

The amount of insurance carried is $60,000.

The amount of insurance required is 0.50 (for 50 percent coinsurance) multiplied by $180,000, which equals $90,000.

The loss amount is $12,000.

Applying the formula:

$60,000 (the amount of insurance carried) divided by $90,000 (the amount of insurance required) multiplied by $12,000 (the loss amount) equals $8,000 (the loss payment from Susan's insurer to her for her business income loss).

Educational Objective 5

5-1. The optional coverages that eliminate or suspend the Coinsurance condition are the Maximum Period of Indemnity, the Monthly Limit of Indemnity, and Business Income Agreed Value.

5-2. Insureds should only add the Maximum Period of Indemnity coverage option to their business income insurance if they are certain that any suspension of operations will last no more than four months.

5-3. To activate the Business Income Agreed Value coverage option, an insurer must take two steps. First, the insurer must secure from the insured a completed business income report/worksheet showing this information:

- The insured's actual data for the most recent twelve-month accounting period before the date of the worksheet

- Estimated data for the twelve months immediately following inception of the coverage

  Second, the insurer must enter the agreed value into the declarations. The agreed value must be at least equal to the product obtained by multiplying the coinsurance percentage shown in the declarations by the estimated net income and operating expenses shown on the worksheet for the twelve months following inception of the optional coverage.

5-4. The Extended Period of Indemnity coverage option extends the Extended Business Income (EBI) additional coverage to include business income losses that continue for more than sixty days after the property is restored. Insureds that own restaurants and clothing stores depend on strong customer relationships and repeat business and are unlikely to return to normal income levels within sixty days of reopening after a severe loss. So for such insureds, this optional coverage can be highly attractive.

5-5. Brad's covered losses will be calculated in these ways:

a. Since Brad's period of restoration is only 90 days, the 120-day restriction of the Maximum Period of Indemnity optional coverage does not apply to this loss. However, the policy limit does. The policy limit of $60,000 is not enough to cover Brad's business income loss of $150,000 ($50,000 per month multiplied by three months). So Brad's insurer will pay up to the policy limit of $60,000.

b. The policy limit of $600,000 is not a limiting factor in determining the amount Brad's insurer will pay because it is high enough to pay the full amount of the loss, $300,000 ($50,000 per month multiplied by six months). However, Brad's period of restoration is 180 days. Therefore, the 120-day restriction of the Maximum Period of Indemnity optional coverage does apply to this loss. Brad's insurer will only pay the business income loss incurred within the first four months of the period of restoration, which equals $200,000 ($50,000 per month multiplied by four months).

5-6. The 90 days of EPI coverage in Sally's policy will cover only three months of Sally's loss of business income after the restaurant resumed operations. Thus, the amount payable by the insurer under EPI is $120,000 (3 × $40,000 = $120,000). However, the amount payable as EPI is also subject to the business income limit of insurance. The amount the insurer paid for business income loss during the period of restoration plus the additional amount covered under EPI ($300,000 + $120,000 = $420,000) is less than the $500,000 limit. Therefore, the insurer will pay the full amount of the covered EPI loss: $120,000.

Educational Objective 6

6-1. These answers address the business income fire loss of Mighty Fine Jewelry:

a. A basic requirement, expressed in the Policy Period and Coverage Territory provision in the Commercial Property Conditions, is that the loss or damage must commence during the policy period shown in the declarations and must commence within the coverage territory in order for coverage to apply. The facts of MFJ's claim satisfy this requirement because the business income loss commenced on December 1, 20X1, which is within the policy period stated in the declarations; and the loss commenced at the described premises, which is within the coverage territory.

b. To be covered under the Business Income insuring agreement, a loss must be actual loss of business income as defined and must meet several requirements imposed by the Business Income insuring agreement. MFJ sustained a rental income loss of $10,000, which is not covered under MFJ's business income coverage because MFJ selected option (2) Business Income Other Than "Rental Value." MFJ may have saved a substantial amount of premium for selecting option (2), but by doing so MFJ chose to retain the losses of rental income when a covered loss occurs.

MFJ also sustained a $4,000 loss of business income, as defined in the Business Income insuring agreement. Because the claim is for business income other than rental income, the loss falls within option (2), Business Income Other Than "Rental Value," shown in the declarations. Furthermore, the circumstances of the claim meet the other requirements imposed by the insuring agreement:

- The actual loss of MFJ's business income was due to the necessary suspension of MFJ's operations.

- The suspension was caused by direct physical loss of or damage to property at the premises described in the declarations.

- The loss or damage was caused by a Covered Cause of Loss.

However, The Business Income insuring agreement states that the insurer will pay actual loss of Business Income only during the "period of restoration." According to the policy definition of this term, the period of restoration, for purposes of Business Income coverage (as opposed to Extra Expense coverage), begins "seventy-two hours after the time of direct physical loss or damage." Because MFJ sustained $4,000 of business income loss during those first seventy-two hours (three days), that amount will not be covered as a business income loss.

Since none of MFJ's business income losses are covered, further analysis using the DICE method and determining the amounts payable are not necessary.

Direct Your Learning

Commercial Crime and Equipment Breakdown Insurance

Educational Objectives

After learning the content of this assignment, you should be able to:

1. Describe the basic characteristics of the ISO commercial crime program and financial institution bonds.

2. Summarize the seven insuring agreements of the Commercial Crime Coverage Form in terms of these elements:
   - Covered causes of loss
   - Covered property
   - Where coverage applies

3. Apply the Commercial Crime Coverage Form's Limit of Insurance and Deductible provisions to a claim.

4. Identify losses that the Commercial Crime Coverage Form excludes.

5. Explain how the Commercial Crime Coverage Form's conditions address each of these issues:
   - Interests insured
   - Where coverage applies
   - When coverage applies
   - Claim-related duties and procedures
   - Conditions applicable to Employee Theft only

6. Given a case, determine whether, and for how much, a described loss would be covered by the Commercial Crime Coverage Form.

4

7. Describe equipment breakdown insurance in terms of these elements:

   - Why equipment breakdown insurance is needed

   - Insuring agreements included in equipment breakdown coverage forms

   - Conditions that distinguish equipment breakdown insurance from other types of insurance

Outline

- **Overview of Commercial Crime Insurance**
  - A. ISO Commercial Crime Program
  - B. Financial Institution Bonds
- **Commercial Crime Insuring Agreements**
  - A. Employee Theft
  - B. Forgery or Alteration
  - C. Inside the Premises—Theft of Money and Securities
  - D. Inside the Premises—Robbery or Safe Burglary of Other Property
  - E. Outside the Premises
  - F. Computer and Funds Transfer Fraud
  - G. Money Orders and Counterfeit Money
- **Commercial Crime Limits and Deductible**
  - A. Limit of Insurance
    1. Definition of Occurrence
    2. Special Limits of Insurance
  - B. Deductible
- **Commercial Crime Exclusions**
  - A. General Exclusions
  - B. Exclusions Applicable Only to Employee Theft
  - C. Exclusions Applicable Only to Inside the Premises and Outside the Premises
  - D. Exclusions Applicable Only to Computer and Funds Transfer Fraud
- **Commercial Crime Conditions**
  - A. Interests Insured
  - B. Where Coverage Applies
  - C. When Coverage Applies
    1. Extended Period to Discover Loss
    2. Loss Sustained During Prior Insurance Issued by Us or Any Affiliate
    3. Loss Sustained During Prior Insurance Not Issued by Us or Any Affiliate
  - D. Claim-Related Duties and Procedures
  - E. Conditions Applicable to Employee Theft Only

- **Determining Whether the Commercial Crime Coverage Form Covers a Loss**
  - A. Case Facts
  - B. Necessary Reference Materials
  - C. Overview of Steps
  - D. Determination of Coverage
    1. DICE Analysis Step 1: Declarations
    2. DICE Analysis Step 2: Insuring Agreement
    3. DICE Analysis Step 3: Conditions
    4. DICE Analysis Step 4: Exclusions
  - E. Determination of Amounts Payable
- **Equipment Breakdown Insurance**
  - A. Need for Equipment Breakdown Insurance
  - B. Insuring Agreements
    1. Property Damage
    2. Expediting Expenses
    3. Business Income and Extra Expense
  - C. Other Insuring Agreements
  - D. Conditions
    1. Suspension
    2. Joint or Disputed Loss Agreement
    3. Jurisdictional Inspections

 Use the SMART Online Practice Exams to test your understanding of the course material. You can review questions over a single assignment or multiple assignments, or you can take an exam over the entire course.

For each assignment, you should define or describe each of the Key Words and Phrases and answer each of the Review and Application Questions.

Educational Objective 1

Describe the basic characteristics of the ISO commercial crime program and financial institution bonds.

Review Questions

1-1. Describe the types of businesses that the Insurance Services Office, Inc. (ISO) commercial crime coverage forms and policy forms are designed to insure.

1-2. Although financial institution bonds are insurance policies, why are they called "bonds"?

Educational Objective 2

Summarize the seven insuring agreements of the Commercial Crime Coverage Form in terms of these elements:

- **Covered causes of loss**
- **Covered property**
- **Where coverage applies**

Review Questions

2-1. Identify the types of property covered under the Employee Theft insuring agreement in the Commercial Crime Coverage Form.

2-2. Identify the types of losses that are paid under the Commercial Crime Coverage Form's Forgery or Alteration insuring agreement.

2-3. Describe the coverage provided by the Inside the Premises—Theft of Money and Securities insuring agreement.

2-4. Describe the coverage provided by the Outside the Premises insuring agreement.

2-5. Describe the coverage that is provided under the Computer and Funds Transfer Fraud insuring agreement.

Application Question

2-6. Fernwood Insurance Agency (FIA) is insured under a Commercial Crime Coverage Form that includes the Employee Theft insuring agreement. Indicate whether FIA's Employee Theft insuring agreement would cover each of these losses. If FIA's employee theft insurance would not cover a loss, explain why.

    a. One of FIA's employees, a bookkeeper, wrote several unauthorized register checks to herself for computer equipment she allegedly purchased for the agency office. Then she tricked FIA's treasurer into signing the checks. The equipment was delivered to her home and was never taken to the agency office.

b. FIA's Systems Department vice president discovered that Hal, of FIA's Information Technology Department, sold one of the computer programs he developed while working for FIA to a competitor, as well as the data associated with that program. The program was owned and copyrighted by FIA.

Educational Objective 3
Apply the Commercial Crime Coverage Form's Limit of Insurance and Deductible provisions to a claim.

Review Questions

3-1. Identify the manner in which the Commercial Crime Coverage Form determines the most the insurer will pay for all loss resulting directly from an "occurrence" (as defined in the policy).

3-2. Identify the portion of the definition of "occurrence" that applies to every commercial crime coverage.

3-3. Describe how the insurer responds under a commercial crime policy if the amount of loss exceeds the deductible.

3-4. Describe the definition of occurrence that applies to forgery or alteration.

Educational Objective 4

Identify losses that the Commercial Crime Coverage Form excludes.

Review Questions

4-1. For each type of loss indicated, identify the exclusion applicable to the Insurance Services Office, Inc. (ISO) Commercial Crime Coverage Form that would eliminate coverage:

a. A company lost $2 million in contracts after an employee sold its secret process to a competitor.

b. A business partner embezzled funds from the partnership's bank account.

c. A business director colluded with friends to offer discounts on memberships, causing the organization to lose $10,000 in membership fees.

4-2. An employee of a business made an accounting error that resulted in a loss of $122,000 by the time the error was discovered. Identify the exclusion in the ISO Commercial Crime Coverage Form that would eliminate coverage for this loss.

4-3. A man used his personal computer and his roommate's company credit card to make an unauthorized electronic purchase of $15,000. Identify the exclusion in the ISO Commercial Crime Coverage Form that would eliminate coverage for this loss.

Application Question

4-4. A bookstore is insured under an ISO Commercial Crime Coverage Form that includes the insuring agreement for Inside the Premises—Theft of Money and Securities. During a burglary, thieves vandalized the bookstore office by smashing several desks and computer monitors. Indicate whether the insuring agreement would cover the damage to the desks and the monitors.

Educational Objective 5

Explain how the Commercial Crime Coverage Form's conditions address each of these issues:

- **Interests insured**
- **Where coverage applies**
- **When coverage applies**
- **Claim-related duties and procedures**
- **Conditions applicable to Employee Theft only**

Review Questions

5-1. Under a loss sustained crime form, describe the operation of these three conditions to determine when a loss must occur in order to be covered.

   a.   Extended Period to Discover Loss

b.   Loss Sustained During Prior Insurance Issued by Us or Any Affiliate

c.   Loss Sustained During Prior Insurance Not Issued by Us or Any Affiliate

5-2.   Under the Valuation—Settlement condition of a crime policy, how is the
value of a covered loss generally determined for each of the three categories of
covered property?

a.   Money

b.   Securities

c. Property other than money and securities that is lost or damaged

5-3. Briefly describe the two parts of the Termination as to Any Employee condition in the commercial crime form.

Application Question

5-4. For nine consecutive years with the same insurer, Emily has insured her souvenir shop under the loss sustained version of the Insurance Services Office, Inc. (ISO) Commercial Crime Coverage Form, which includes the Employee Theft insuring agreement. During the ninth year of coverage, she learned that her staff accountant, Jerome, had been embezzling funds in July (her peak season) for each of the last six years. Identify which condition determines whether Emily's crime form covers this loss, and explain which policy covers the loss and why.

Educational Objective 6

Given a case, determine whether, and for how much, a described loss would be covered by the Commercial Crime Coverage Form.

Application Questions

6-1. TAF is a second-hand appliance and furniture store. TAF purchased an annual commercial package policy that includes Insurance Services Office's (ISO's) Commercial Crime Coverage Form (Loss Sustained Form). TAF decided not to insure its employee theft exposure because management believed its staff was honest. TAF selected these insuring agreements, each with a $1,000 deductible: Inside the Premises—Theft of Money and Securities with a limit of $30,000, and Outside the Premises with a limit of $30,000. The policy effective date is March 1, 20X0.

On January 31, 20X1, TAF discovered that merchandise valued at $5,000 was missing from inventory. Dennis, a manager, admitted that he had colluded with TAF's delivery contractor to deliver the missing appliances and furniture to his own home.

Given the facts presented in the case and assuming that no endorsements to TAF's policy affect the coverage in the loss and all policy conditions were met, use the DICE method to determine whether the commercial crime form will cover the loss. The declarations confirm that coverage was in force.

a. Which one of the insuring agreements would apply to the loss of $5,000 of merchandise?

b. The policy conditions were met, but which one of the exclusions eliminates coverage for this loss?

6-2. Country Style Kitchen, Inc. (CSK) is a restaurant. At closing time, the manager on duty counts the cash, checks, and credit card receipts in the cash register. The manager leaves $1,000 in the register drawer and prepares a deposit. During any shift, a cashier, the receptionist, the manager, and any of the waitresses are allowed access to the cash drawer.

CSK purchased an annual commercial package policy that includes ISO's Commercial Crime Coverage Form (Loss Sustained Form). CSK selected these insuring agreements, each with a $1,000 deductible: Employee Theft with a limit of $100,000, Inside the Premises—Theft of Money and Securities with a limit of $20,000, and Outside the Premises with a limit of $20,000.

Four months after the crime coverage was in force, a manager caught a waitress, Janelle, stealing $1,500 from the register drawer.

a. Given the facts presented in the case, use the DICE method to determine whether the commercial crime form will cover the loss. Assume no endorsements to CSK's policy affect the coverage in the loss; the insured reported each loss to its crime insurer promptly after discovering it, cooperated with the insurer, and maintained records of all property covered under the policy; and no exclusions apply. The declarations confirm that coverage was in force. If the loss is covered, identify the insuring agreement that would provide coverage and the amount the insurer would pay for the loss. If the loss is not covered, explain the reason.

b. CSK's general manager decided to give Janelle another chance and did not fire her. Six months after the first loss, Janelle was caught stealing $900 from the cash register. Explain why CSK's crime policy would not cover this loss.

Educational Objective 7

Describe equipment breakdown insurance in terms of these elements:

- **Why equipment breakdown insurance is needed**
- **Insuring agreements included in equipment breakdown coverage forms**
- **Conditions that distinguish equipment breakdown insurance from other types of insurance**

Review Questions

7-1. What gaps in the commercial property causes of loss forms is filled by equipment breakdown insurance?

7-2. What types of equipment malfunctions that cause direct physical damage to covered equipment are included in the form definition of "breakdown"?

7-3. Identify and explain the condition in the equipment breakdown form that enables the insurer to act immediately when imminent danger of an accident exists.

Application Question

7-4. A power plant operated by a public utility, SPT, was shut down for twelve days for repairs following a fierce electrical storm. Customers in that area were without power for twelve days. INDI Manufacturing was an SPT customer and was forced to shut down its operation until power was restored. But after power returned, its manufacturing equipment remained unavailable for three days because it was damaged by the electrical failure and needed repair. Even though no other damage to the plant occurred, INDI could not produce the inventory needed to maintain its regular revenues. Identify three insuring agreements available in an equipment breakdown policy that would have benefited INDI and briefly explain what would be covered in them.

Answers to Assignment 4 Questions

NOTE: These answers are provided to give students a basic understanding of acceptable types of responses. They often are not the only valid answers and are not intended to provide an exhaustive response to the questions.

Educational Objective 1

1-1. The ISO commercial crime coverage forms and policy forms are designed for insuring any type of nongovernment commercial or not-for-profit entity other than a financial institution.

1-2. Financial institution bonds are called "bonds" because one of the key coverages that they provide is employee dishonesty insurance, which was traditionally called a "fidelity bond."

Educational Objective 2

2-1. The Commercial Crime Coverage Form Employee Theft insuring agreement covers, as defined in the policy, money, securities, and all other tangible property that has intrinsic value.

2-2. The Forgery or Alteration insuring agreement pays losses of the insured or its representatives resulting from forgery or alteration of checks and similar instruments; it does not pay losses resulting from the insured's knowing acceptance of instruments that have been forged or altered by others.

2-3. The Inside the Premises—Theft of Money and Securities insuring agreement covers money and securities inside the "premises" or a "banking premises" against theft, disappearance, or destruction.

2-4. The Outside the Premises insuring agreement covers money, securities, and other property while outside the premises and in the care and custody of either a "messenger" or an armored vehicle company.

2-5. The first part of the Computer and Funds Transfer Fraud insuring agreement covers loss resulting directly from fraudulent entry of electronic data or computer program into, or change of electronic data or computer program within, a computer system owned, leased, or operated by the named insured. The second part of the insuring agreement covers loss resulting directly from a fraudulent instruction directing a financial institution to debit the named insured's transfer account and transfer, pay, or deliver money or securities from that account.

2-6. FIA's coverage under a Commercial Crime Coverage Form that includes the Employee Theft insuring agreement provides these coverages:

   a. Unauthorized register checks signed by the treasurer would qualify as "money." Therefore, theft by an employee of those checks would be covered.

   b. Hal's unlawful taking of the computer program and associated data would not be covered under FIA's Employee Theft insuring agreement because the policy definition of "other property" excludes intangible items such as computer programs and electronic data.

Educational Objective 3

3-1.   The Commercial Crime Coverage Form's Limit of Insurance provision states that the most the insurer will pay for all loss resulting directly from an "occurrence" (as defined in the policy) is the applicable limit shown in the declarations.

3-2.   The portion of the definition of "occurrence" that applies to every commercial crime coverage is that "occurrence" includes an individual act, the combined total of all separate acts (whether or not related), or a series of acts (whether or not related).

3-3.   Under a commercial crime policy, if the amount of loss exceeds the deductible, the insurer will pay the amount of the loss in excess of the deductible, up to the limit of insurance.

3-4.   The definition of occurrence that applies to forgery or alteration requires that the act or acts must be committed by a person acting alone or in collusion with others and must involve one or more instruments.

Educational Objective 4

4-1.   These answers identify the exclusions that would eliminate coverage for these losses:

a.   The Confidential or Personal Information exclusion would eliminate coverage for this type of loss.

b.   The Acts Committed by You, Your Partners or Your Members exclusion would eliminate coverage for this type of loss.

c.   The Acts Committed by Your Employees, Managers, Directors, Trustees or Representatives exclusion would eliminate coverage for this type of loss.

4-2.   The Commercial Crime Coverage Form Accounting or Arithmetical Errors or Omissions exclusion eliminates coverage for the employee's error.

4-3.   The Credit Card Transactions exclusion eliminates coverage for the fraudulent use of a credit card.

4-4.   A Commercial Crime Coverage Form that includes the insuring agreement for Inside the Premises—Theft of Money and Securities would not cover the loss, because vandalism is excluded under that insuring agreement.

Educational Objective 5

5-1.   These answers describe the operation of these three conditions:

a.   The insurer will pay for loss that the named insured sustains through acts committed or events occurring during the policy period and discovered during the policy period or within one year after the policy is canceled. However, the discovery period terminates immediately as of the effective date of any other insurance that the insured obtains that replaces coverage in whole or in part.

   b. The insurer agrees to pay a loss that meets these criteria:

- The loss is discovered during the policy period shown in the declarations.

- The loss occurred while prior insurance, issued by the same insurer or an affiliated insurer, was in effect.

- The current insurance became effective when the prior insurance was canceled.

- The loss would have been covered by the present insurance if the insurance had been in force at the time of loss.

   c. Under this condition, if the prior insurance was not provided by the current insurer or an affiliate, the insurer agrees to pay a loss that meets all of these criteria:

- The loss is discovered during the policy period shown in the declarations.

- The loss occurred while prior insurance, issued by another unaffiliated insurer, was in effect.

- The current insurance became effective when the prior insurance was canceled or terminated.

- The loss would have been covered by the present insurance if the insurance had been in force at the time of loss.

5-2. These answers explain how the value of a covered loss is generally determined for these three categories of covered property:

   a. Money is valued at its face value.

   b. Securities are valued as of the close of business on the day the loss is discovered.

   c. When other property is lost or damaged, the insurer has the option of paying the replacement cost of the property, repairing the property, or replacing it.

5-3. The first part of the Termination as to Any Employee condition automatically terminates employee theft coverage with respect to any employee who has committed a dishonest act as soon as the act is known to the insured or any partner, officer, or director not in collusion with the employee. The second part of the condition gives the insurer the right to cancel coverage with respect to any employee by providing thirty days advance notice to the insured.

5-4. The Loss Sustained During Prior Insurance Issued by Us or Any Affiliate condition would apply to this loss. The insurer agrees to pay a loss (that would be covered by the present insurance) that is discovered during the policy period and occurred while prior insurance issued by the same insurer was in effect. Therefore, these losses can be covered (up to the policy limit) by the policy currently in effect.

Educational Objective 6

6-1. These answers address questions regarding TAF's commercial crime case:

   a. The Employee Theft insuring agreement would apply to this loss; however, TAF chose not to purchase that agreement.

b. The Acts of Employees, Managers, Directors, Trustees or Representatives exclusion applies to losses under all insuring agreements, except for loss covered under the Employee Theft insuring agreement. Because TAF did not purchase the Employee Theft insuring agreement, coverage is excluded for this loss.

6-2. These answers address questions regarding CSK's commercial crime case:

a. The Employee Theft insuring agreement would cover this loss. The conditions were met, and no exclusions applied. The $1,500 loss amount is within the limit for the Employee Theft insuring agreement coverage ($100,000). The insurer would reduce the loss payment by the $1,000 deductible, so the loss payment would be $500 ($1,500 loss – $1,000 deductible).

b. The Termination As to Any Employee condition, which applies only to the Employee Theft insuring agreement, terminates employee theft coverage with respect to any employee who has committed a dishonest act as soon as the act is known to the insured. This condition would preclude coverage for Janelle's repeated theft, so the loss would not be covered by the crime policy.

Educational Objective 7

7-1. The commercial property causes of loss forms exclude electrical breakdown, mechanical breakdown, and steam boiler explosion. Equipment breakdown insurance fills these gaps by covering physical damage to covered equipment and other property of the insured that results from the accidental breakdown of covered equipment.

7-2. The form definition of "breakdown" includes malfunctions such as failure of pressure or vacuum equipment; mechanical failure, including rupturing or bursting caused by centrifugal force; and electrical failure, including arcing.

7-3. The Suspension condition in the equipment breakdown form allows the insurer to immediately suspend equipment breakdown insurance on an item of equipment that the insurer determines to be in a dangerous condition. The insurer can suspend coverage by delivering or mailing a written notice of coverage suspension to the named insured.

7-4. In the power plant scenario presented, these three equipment breakdown policy insuring agreements would benefit INDI:

- The Property Damage insuring agreement would pay for repairs to the manufacturing equipment caused by the electrical failure.

- The Business Income and Extra Expense insuring agreement would replace INDIs lost income and any extra expenses it incurred as a result of the equipment breakdown.

- The Utility Interruption insuring agreement extends the business income and extra expense coverage to include loss sustained by the insured because of breakdown of equipment owned by a utility or other supplier that has contracted to provide the insured with any of these services: electricity, communications, air conditioning, heating, gas, sewer, water, or steam.

B

Direct Your Learning ▶▶

Inland and Ocean Marine Insurance

Educational Objectives

After learning the content of this assignment, you should be able to:

1. Describe inland marine insurance in terms of these elements:
   - The role of the Nationwide Marine Definition
   - The distinction between filed and nonfiled classes of inland marine business
   - The role of judgment rating

2. Summarize the key provisions of each of these traditionally nonfiled classes of inland marine insurance:
   - Contractors equipment
   - Builders risk
   - Transit
   - Motor truck cargo liability
   - Difference in conditions
   - Electronic data processing (EDP) equipment
   - Bailees
   - Instrumentalities of transportation and communication

3. Describe what is covered by each of the filed classes of inland marine insurance.

4. Describe ocean marine insurance in terms of the following elements:
   - The types of loss exposures that can be covered
   - The role of judgment rating

5

5. Summarize the key provisions of these three main types of ocean marine insurance:

   - Cargo insurance

   - Hull insurance

   - Protection and indemnity insurance

6. Given a case describing an organization's loss exposures, recommend appropriate types of inland and ocean marine insurance.

Outline

▶ **Overview of Inland Marine Insurance**
  A. Nationwide Marine Definition
  B. Filed and Nonfiled Classes of Business
  C. Role of Judgment Rating

▶ **Nonfiled Classes of Inland Marine Insurance**
  A. Contractors Equipment
  B. Builders Risk
  C. Transit
  D. Motor Truck Cargo Liability
  E. Difference in Conditions
  F. Electronic Data Processing Equipment
  G. Bailees
  H. Instrumentalities of Transportation and Communication

▶ **Filed Classes of Inland Marine Insurance**
  A. Commercial Articles
  B. Camera and Musical Instrument Dealers
  C. Equipment Dealers
  D. Physicians and Surgeons Equipment
  E. Signs
  F. Theatrical Property
  G. Film
  H. Floor Plan
  I. Jewelers Block
  J. Mail
  K. Accounts Receivable
  L. Valuable Papers and Records

▶ **Overview of Ocean Marine Insurance**
  A. Ocean Marine Loss Exposures
  B. The Role of Judgment Rating in Ocean Marine Insurance

▶ **Ocean Marine Insurance Policies**
  A. Cargo Insurance
    1. Warehouse to Warehouse Clause
    2. Covered Causes of Loss
    3. Valuation of Property
  B. Hull Insurance
  C. Protection and Indemnity Insurance

▶ **Recommending Inland and Ocean Marine Coverages**
  A. Case Facts
  B. Overview of Steps
  C. Identify RBC's Loss Exposures That Can Be Covered by Inland or Ocean Marine Insurance
  D. Consider the Available Types of Inland and Ocean Marine Insurance
  E. Recommend the Most Appropriate Types of Inland and Ocean Marine Insurance

 The SMART Online Practice Exams can be tailored to cover specific assignments, so you can focus your studies on topics you want to master.

For each assignment, you should define or describe each of the Key Words and Phrases and answer each of the Review and Application Questions.

Educational Objective 1

Describe inland marine insurance in terms of these elements:

- **The role of the Nationwide Marine Definition**
- **The distinction between filed and nonfiled classes of inland marine business**
- **The role of judgment rating**

Key Words and Phrases

Inland marine insurance

Marine insurance

Nationwide Marine Definition

Review Questions

1-1. For what reason do states continue to use the updated Nationwide Marine Definition?

1-2. Distinguish between the characteristics of filed classes of inland marine and those of nonfiled classes.

1-3. Explain inland marine underwriters' use of judgment rating.

Educational Objective 2
Summarize the key provisions of each of these traditionally nonfiled classes of inland marine insurance:

- **Contractors equipment**
- **Builders risk**
- **Transit**
- **Motor truck cargo liability**
- **Difference in conditions**
- **Electronic data processing (EDP) equipment**
- **Bailees**
- **Instrumentalities of transportation and communication**

Key Words and Phrases
Contractors equipment floater

Builders risk policy

Motor truck cargo liability policy

Difference in conditions (DIC) policy, or DIC insurance

Review Questions

2-1. What is the purpose of the rental reimbursement coverage that is often added by endorsement to contractors equipment floaters?

2-2. What property does an inland marine builders risk policy typically cover other than the building under construction?

2-3. Describe the coverage territory of many annual transit policies.

2-4. What are the reasons for buying a difference in conditions (DIC) policy?

Application Question

2-5. Identify the type of nonfiled inland marine insurance policy that would provide coverage for each of the following loss exposures:

   a.   A construction company owns several pieces of mobile equipment that remain at a construction site until the construction project is completed.

   b.   A manufacturing company regularly uses its own trucks to deliver finished products to customers.

   c.   A computer services company owns several computers that it uses to develop software packages for local businesses.

   d.   Smith Warehouse needs legal liability coverage for the property of others being stored with Smith.

e.   Ian owns a dry cleaning business and wants to cover customers' goods without regard to his legal liability.

Educational Objective 3

Describe what is covered by each of the filed classes of inland marine insurance.

Review Questions

3-1.   What types of property, other than the insured's professional equipment, materials, supplies, and books, can be insured under the Physicians and Surgeons Equipment Coverage Form?

3-2.   Why do businesses need the coverage provided under the Signs Coverage Form?

3-3. What coverage is provided by the filed Jewelers Block Coverage Form?

Application Question

3-4. Identify a filed inland marine coverage form that would be appropriate for each of these situations:

a. A medical doctor who treats homebound patients needs a policy to cover the contents of her medical bag.

b. A store owner wants to insure his business records because he is concerned that damage to these records will make him unable to collect outstanding debts.

c. A professional photographer needs coverage for his cameras and other equipment.

Educational Objective 4

Describe ocean marine insurance in terms of the following elements:

- **The types of loss exposures that can be covered**
- **The role of judgment rating**

Key Words and Phrases

Cargo insurance

Hull insurance

Protection and indemnity (P&I) insurance

Review Questions

4-1. What property loss exposures do vessel owners face that can be covered by hull insurance?

4-2. When rating hull and protection and indemnity (P&I) insurance, what factors influence the judgment of underwriters?

Educational Objective 5

Summarize the key provisions of these three main types of ocean marine insurance:

- **Cargo insurance**
- **Hull insurance**
- **Protection and indemnity insurance**

Key Word or Phrase

General average

Review Questions

5-1. How does a voyage cargo policy differ from an open cargo policy?

5-2. Explain how each of these clauses affects the coverage provided in a cargo policy:

   a.   Warehouse to warehouse clause

b.   Sue and labor clause

5-3.   What causes of loss are typically covered in a hull insurance policy?

5-4.   Explain how property is normally valued under a hull policy.

5-5.   How does the collision liability clause affect the coverage provided by a hull policy?

5-6.   What types of claims may be covered by protection and indemnity (P&I) insurance?

Application Question

5-7. The *Steamer* is a vessel used to carry cargo for other parties under shipping contracts. The *Steamer* is insured under a hull policy, which contains a collision liability clause, and a P&I policy. As the *Steamer* was leaving harbor, the captain's steering error caused the vessel to collide with another vessel, the *Piston*. The collision caused damage to both vessels and their cargoes. Three crew members on the *Steamer* were injured. Which of the two policies covering the *Steamer* will cover these losses that resulted from the collision?

a.   Damage to the *Steamer*

b.   Damage to the *Piston*

c.   Damage to cargo owned by others aboard the *Steamer*

d.   Damage to cargo aboard the *Piston*

e.   Bodily injury to the three crew members on the *Steamer*

Educational Objective 6
Given a case describing an organization's loss exposures, recommend appropriate types of inland and ocean marine insurance.

Key Word or Phrase

Retention

Application Question

6-1.   Satellite Sharing Techs (SST), a television satellite dish supplier, owns an office building, twenty units of mobile equipment, a fleet of trucks, materials for installing satellite receiving equipment, satellite receivers, laptop computers, and a shop for storage.

SST purchases all its materials and equipment from suppliers located in the United States. These items are delivered by motor carriers to SST's shop and SST, as opposed to its suppliers, bears the risk of loss to a shipment during transit.

SST employs technicians who install and repair customers' and their leased equipment at customers' locations and in its shop. Depending on the circumstances of each loss, SST could be held legally liable for damage to customers' equipment while it is in SST's care, custody, or control.

When answering the questions in this case-based activity, consider only the information supported by the facts of the case.

a. What property loss exposure(s) could SST insure under ocean or inland marine coverages?

b. What liability loss exposure(s) could SST insure under ocean or inland marine coverages?

c. SST's only loss exposure that can be covered by more than one type of inland marine coverage is its exposure to property in transit by motor carriers. Assuming that SST ships on an occasional basis, which coverage would best meet its needs? Explain your answer.

d. For each of SST's remaining loss exposures, which inland marine coverage would you recommend?

Answers to Assignment 5 Questions

NOTE: These answers are provided to give students a basic understanding of acceptable types of responses. They often are not the only valid answers and are not intended to provide an exhaustive response to the questions.

Educational Objective 1

1-1. States continue to use the updated Nationwide Marine Definition to determine whether a particular coverage is marine insurance (either inland or ocean) under their form and rate filing laws. Typically, commercial inland and ocean marine insurance is subject to less rate and form regulation than other lines of insurance.

1-2. Filed classes of inland marine are characterized by a large number of potential insureds and reasonably homogeneous loss exposures. Nonfiled classes are characterized by a relatively small number of potential insureds, diverse loss exposures, or both.

1-3. Judgment rating is used by underwriters to rate one-of-a-kind risks. Judgment rating requires a thorough knowledge of the class of business for which coverage is being written. An inland marine underwriter might have to draw on expertise in any of several specialized fields—fine arts, heavy equipment, construction, or communications—to determine an adequate rate for the unique risks that are eligible for coverage.

Educational Objective 2

2-1. Rental reimbursement coverage, often added by endorsement to contractors equipment floaters, pays the cost of renting substitute equipment when covered property has been put out of service by a covered cause of loss.

2-2. Other than the building under construction, an inland marine builders risk policy typically covers temporary structures at the building site and building materials while on the insured location, in transit, or in storage at another location.

2-3. The coverage territory of many annual transit policies only includes the continental United States, Alaska, and Canada, including airborne shipments between these places.

2-4. These are the reasons for buying a difference in conditions (DIC) policy:

- To provide coverage for flood and earthquake exposures not covered by basic policies

- To provide excess limits over flood and earthquake coverages included in basic policies

- To cover loss exposures not covered in basic policies, such as property in transit or loss of business income resulting from theft or transit losses

- To cover property at overseas locations

2-5. Coverage would be provided for the following loss exposures by the specified types of nonfiled inland marine insurance:

a. The construction company's owned mobile equipment at a construction site would be covered by a contractors equipment floater.

b. The manufacturing company regularly using its own trucks to deliver finished products to customers would be covered by an annual transit policy.

c. The computer services company would be covered by an electronic data processing (EDP) equipment floater.

d. As the insured bailee, Smith Warehouse can obtain legal liability coverage for property of others through a warehouse operator's legal liability policy.

e. The dry cleaning business would be covered by a bailees' customers policy.

Educational Objective 3

3-1. The Physicians and Surgeons Equipment Coverage Form covers the insured's office equipment and (if the insured is a tenant) improvements and betterments that the insured has made to a leased building.

3-2. The Signs Coverage Form is used by many businesses because commercial property forms severely limit coverage for signs.

3-3. The filed Jewelers Block Coverage Form covers damage to the insured's stock of jewelry, precious and semiprecious stones, watches, precious metals, and similar merchandise, along with other stock used in a retail jeweler's business, including similar property of others in the insured's care, custody, or control.

3-4. Coverage appropriate for the following situations would be provided by these specified types of filed inland marine insurance:

a. The contents of the doctor's medical bag would be covered by the Physicians and Surgeons Equipment Coverage Form.

b. The store owner's business record would be covered by the Accounts Receivable Coverage Form.

c. The professional photographer's cameras and equipment would be covered by the Commercial Articles Coverage Form.

Educational Objective 4

4-1. Vessel owners face the possibility that their vessels could be damaged or destroyed by fire, war, breakage of machinery, the action of wind and waves, the striking of rocks or other vessels, and the shifting of cargo.

4-2. Hull and P&I insurance underwriters consider past loss experience; the size, type, and age of the insured vessel; the area of navigation; the trade in which the vessel is employed; the nation in which the vessel is registered; and the vessel owner's reputation and quality of management.

Educational Objective 5

5-1. A voyage policy covers cargo for a single trip specified in the policy. An open cargo policy covers all goods shipped or received by the insured during the policy's term.

5-2.   The coverage provided in a cargo policy is affected by these clauses as described:

a.   The warehouse to warehouse clause covers the insured cargo during the ordinary course of transit from the time the cargo leaves the point of shipment until it is delivered to its final destination, including inland transit.

b.   The sue and labor clause covers the cost of reasonable measures that the insured is required to take to protect property from damage at the time of a loss.

5-3.   A hull insurance policy typically covers these causes of loss:

- Perils of the seas

- Fire, lightning, and earthquake

- Barratry

- All other like perils

If the policy includes the additional perils clause, it also covers several other perils, including electrical breakdown, bursting of boilers, breakage of shafts, latent defects, and negligence of the crew.

5-4.   Under a hull policy, a vessel is normally insured for a value agreed on by the insurer and the insured. For a total loss, the insurer pays the agreed value. For a partial loss, the insurer pays the cost of repairs.

5-5.   Collision liability coverage is a separate amount of insurance covering the insured's liability for collision damage to other vessels and their cargoes. Liability for bodily injury from the collision is not covered. Defense costs are covered in addition to the limit of collision liability insurance.

5-6.   P&I insurance may cover vessel owners for these types of liability claims:

- Damage to bridges, piers, wharves, and other structures along waterways

- Injury to passengers, crew, and other persons on the insured vessel

- Injury to persons on other vessels

- Damage to cargo of others aboard the insured vessel

5-7.   These answers indicate which of the two policies will apply to each loss:

a.   The hull policy will cover damage to the *Steamer*.

b.   Damage to the *Piston* will be covered under the hull policy's collision liability clause.

c.   The P&I policy will cover damage to the cargo owned by others aboard the *Steamer*.

d.   Damage to the cargo aboard the *Piston* will be covered under the collision liability clause of the hull policy.

e.   The injuries to the crew members will be covered by the P&I policy.

Educational Objective 6

6-1. These answers apply to the SST case:

    a. SST has no property loss exposures that could be insured under ocean marine coverages, but these loss exposures could be insured under inland marine coverages: mobile equipment; materials for installing satellite receiving equipment and satellite receivers; property in transit by motor carriers; and office computers and laptops, software, and electronic data.

    b. SST has no liability loss exposures that could be insured under ocean marine coverages. Its only liability loss exposure that could be insured under inland marine coverage is its liability for damage to customers' equipment in its care, custody, or control.

    c. Because SST ships on an occasional basis, trip transit policies for each shipment would be more cost-effective than an annual transit policy.

    d. These inland marine coverages are recommended for each of SST's remaining loss exposures: a contractors equipment floater for its mobile equipment exposure; an instrumentalities of transportation and communication policy for its exposure of materials for installing satellite receiving equipment and satellite receivers; an electronic data processing equipment floater for its exposure to office computers and laptops, software, and electronic data; and a bailees' customers policy for its exposure to liability for damage to customer's equipment in its care, custody, or control.

Direct Your Learning

Commercial General Liability Insurance, Part I

Educational Objectives

After learning the content of this assignment, you should be able to:

1. Describe commercial general liability insurance in terms of these elements:

   - The types of losses that can be covered by general liability insurance

   - The components of a commercial general liability coverage part

2. Determine whether a described claim meets the conditions imposed by the Coverage A insuring agreement of the Commercial General Liability Coverage Form (occurrence version).

3. Determine whether any of the exclusions applicable to Coverage A of the Commercial General Liability Coverage Form eliminate coverage for a described claim.

4. Determine whether a described claim meets the conditions imposed by the Coverage B insuring agreement of the Commercial General Liability Coverage Form and whether any of the Coverage B exclusions eliminate coverage for the claim.

5. Determine whether a described claim meets the conditions imposed by the Coverage C insuring agreement of the Commercial General Liability Coverage Form and whether any of the Coverage C exclusions eliminate coverage for the claim.

6. Summarize the supplementary payments of the Commercial General Liability Coverage Form.

Outline

▶ **Overview of Commercial General Liability Insurance**

A. Bodily Injury and Property Damage Liability

   1. Premises and Operations

   2. Products and Completed Operations

B. Personal and Advertising Injury Liability

C. Medical Payments

D. Other General Liability Exposures

E. Components of a General Liability Coverage Part

   1. General Liability Declarations

   2. General Liability Coverage Forms

   3. Endorsements

▶ **CGL Coverage A—Insuring Agreement**

A. Insurer's Duty to Pay Damages

   1. Legally Obligated (Legally Liable) to Pay Damages

   2. Bodily Injury and Property Damage

   3. Injury or Damage to Which the Insurance Applies

   4. Caused by an Occurrence

   5. Coverage Territory

   6. Injury or Damage Occurring During the Policy Period

   7. Injury or Damage Not Known Before the Policy Period

B. Insurer's Duty to Defend

▶ **CGL Coverage A—Exclusions**

A. Expected or Intended Injury

B. Contractual Liability

C. Liquor Liability

D. Workers Compensation and Employers Liability

E. Pollution

F. Aircraft, Auto, or Watercraft

G. Mobile Equipment

H. War

I. Damage to Property

J. Insured's Products and Work

   1. Damage to Your Product

   2. Damage to Your Work

   3. Damage to Impaired Property or Property Not Physically Injured

   4. Recall of Products, Work, or Impaired Property

K. Personal and Advertising Injury

L. Electronic Data

M. Recording and Distribution of Material or Information in Violation of Law

N. Fire Legal Liability Coverage

▶ **CGL Coverage B—Personal and Advertising Injury Liability**

A. Coverage B Insuring Agreement

B. Coverage B Exclusions

   1. Knowing Violation of Rights of Another

   2. Material Published With Knowledge of Falsity

   3. Material Published Prior to Policy Period

   4. Criminal Acts

   5. Contractual Liability

   6. Breach of Contract

   7. Quality or Performance of Goods—Failure to Conform to Statements

   8. Wrong Description of Prices

   9. Infringement of Copyright, Patent, Trademark, or Trade Secret

   10. Insureds in Media and Internet-Type Businesses

   11. Electronic Chatrooms or Bulletin Boards

   12. Unauthorized Use of Another's Name or Product

   13. Pollution

   14. Pollution-Related

   15. War

   16. Recording and Distribution of Material or Information in Violation of Law

▶ **CGL Coverage C—Medical Payments**

A. Coverage C Insuring Agreement

B. Coverage C Exclusions

▶ **CGL Supplementary Payments**

s.m.a.r.t. tips When you take the randomized full practice exams in the SMART Online Practice Exams product, you are seeing the same kinds of questions you will see when you take the actual exam.

For each assignment, you should define or describe each of the Key Words and Phrases and answer each of the Review and Application Questions.

Educational Objective 1

Describe commercial general liability insurance in terms of these elements:

- **The types of losses that can be covered by general liability insurance**
- **The components of a commercial general liability coverage part**

Review Questions

1-1. What are the two broad categories of liability loss insured under Coverage A and Coverage B of the Commercial General Liability (CGL) Coverage Form?

1-2. What is the premises and operations liability exposure?

1-3. What is the products and completed operations liability exposure?

1-4. Give three examples of personal and advertising injury liability offenses covered by the CGL form.

1-5. Under Coverage C—Medical Payments of the CGL form, what must occur for medical expenses to be covered?

1-6. What are the components of a general liability coverage part in a commercial package policy?

Educational Objective 2

Determine whether a described claim meets the conditions imposed by the Coverage A insuring agreement of the Commercial General Liability Coverage Form (occurrence version).

Review Questions

2-1. Identify the seven conditions the occurrence version of the commercial general liability (CGL) policy insuring agreement imposes on the insurer's duty to pay damages.

2-2. Identify and describe the three basic types of damages a court might award.

2-3. Identify both elements included in the CGL policy's definition of property damage.

2-4. Identify the CGL policy's coverage territory.

2-5. Explain what proceedings, other than formal lawsuits, are included in the CGL definition of "suit."

Educational Objective 3

Determine whether any of the exclusions applicable to Coverage A of the Commercial General Liability Coverage Form eliminate coverage for a described claim.

Review Questions

3-1. Explain how Coverage A of the Commercial General Liability (CGL) Coverage Form would cover bodily injury resulting from the use of reasonable force to protect persons or property.

3-2. Explain why the CGL policy's Pollution exclusion is worded broadly.

3-3. Identify the two general categories of loss for which the CGL's Mobile Equipment exclusion eliminates coverage.

3-4. Identify examples of items for which the CGL policy's Damage to Property exclusion eliminates coverage.

3-5. Identify the purpose of the CGL policy's exclusions related to the insured's products and work.

Educational Objective 4

Determine whether a described claim meets the conditions imposed by the Coverage B insuring agreement of the Commercial General Liability Coverage Form and whether any of the Coverage B exclusions eliminate coverage for the claim.

Review Questions

4-1.   Identify examples of the offenses that the Commercial General Liability (CGL) Coverage Form defines as personal and advertising injury.

4-2.   Identify the CGL exclusion that would apply if an insured knowingly uses a competitor's advertising ideas in his or her own advertisements

4-3.   Describe the CGL policy's Contractual Liability exclusion.

4-4.   An insured who is an auto dealer advertises a new car for $3,399 instead of its actual price of $33,999. When the insured refuses to sell the car for the advertised amount, several potential buyers sue for the $30,600 difference between the actual price and the advertised price. Identify the CGL policy exclusion that applies in this circumstance.

4-5.   Identify the primary difference between the CGL Coverage A and Coverage B Pollution exclusions.

Educational Objective 5

Determine whether a described claim meets the conditions imposed by the Coverage C insuring agreement of the Commercial General Liability Coverage Form and whether any of the Coverage C exclusions eliminate coverage for the claim.

Review Questions

5-1.   What does the insurer agree to pay under the Commercial General Liability (CGL) Coverage Form Coverage C insuring agreement?

5-2. Identify the categories of persons excluded from the CGL policy's medical payments coverage.

5-3. Explain why the medical payments coverage provided by the CGL's policy's Coverage C is not considered liability insurance.

Educational Objective 6

Summarize the supplementary payments of the Commercial General Liability Coverage Form.

Key Words and Phrases

Prejudgment interest

Postjudgment interest

Review Questions

6-1. Which commercial general liability (CGL) policy insuring agreements are supplemented by the supplementary payments section?

6-2. Are the supplementary payments subject to the limits of insurance that apply to CGL coverage?

6-3. Identify three supplementary payments included in the CGL coverage form.

Application Question

6-4. Amelia owns a tattoo parlor and insures her business with a CGL policy. Recently, Amelia was sued by a customer who developed a skin infection after receiving a new tattoo. The case went to court, and Amelia's insurer asked her to testify. Amelia missed three days of work for the trial and suffered lost income as a result. How much will Amelia's CGL policy compensate her, if at all, for loss of earnings?

Answers to Assignment 6 Questions

NOTE: These answers are provided to give students a basic understanding of acceptable types of responses. They often are not the only valid answers and are not intended to provide an exhaustive response to the questions.

Educational Objective 1

1-1. The two broad categories insured under Coverage A and Coverage B of the CGL form are these:

* Bodily injury and property damage liability

* Personal and advertising injury liability

1-2. The premises and operations liability exposure is the possibility that an organization will be held liable because of bodily injury or property damage caused by an accident that either occurs on the organization's premises or arises out of the organization's ongoing (as opposed to completed) operations on or off those premises.

1-3. The products and completed operations liability exposure is the possibility that an organization will be held liable because of bodily injury or property damage caused by an accident arising out of products manufactured, sold, or distributed by the organization and occurring after the products are no longer on the organization's premises or in the organization's physical possession or by an accident arising out of the organization's completed work, including defective parts or materials furnished with the work.

1-4. Examples of personal and advertising injury liability offenses covered by the CGL form include false arrest, wrongful eviction, libel, slander, and infringement upon another's copyright in the insured's advertisement.

1-5. To be covered by the CGL form, medical expenses must result from bodily injury because of an accident occurring on the insured's premises or arising out of the insured's operations (other than completed operations) anywhere in the coverage territory.

1-6. The components of a general liability coverage part in a commercial package policy are these:

* One or more general liability declarations forms

* One or more general liability coverage forms

* Any applicable endorsements

Educational Objective 2

2-1. In the occurrence version of the CGL, the insuring agreement imposes seven conditions on the insurer's duty to pay damages:

- The insured must be legally obligated (legally liable) to pay damages.

- The damages must result from bodily injury or property damage as defined in the policy.

- The policy must apply to the bodily injury or property damage.

- The bodily injury or property damage must be caused by an occurrence.

- The occurrence must take place in the coverage territory.

- The bodily injury or property damage must occur during the policy period. (The claims-made form contains a different provision in this regard.)

- The bodily injury or property damage must not be known to the named insured or certain other persons before the policy period.

2-2. The basic types of damages a court might award include these:

- Special damages, for such out-of-pocket costs such as medical expenses and loss of earnings

- General damages, for such intangibles as pain and suffering

- Punitive damages, to punish or make an example of the wrongdoer

2-3. The CGL policy's definition of property damage includes these two elements:

- Physical injury to tangible property, including resulting loss of use of that property

- Loss of use of tangible property that is not physically injured

2-4. The CGL policy's coverage territory that applies to most claims is the United States (including its territories and possessions), Puerto Rico, and Canada. Other international waters and airspace are included in the coverage territory if the injury or damage occurs in the course of travel or transportation to or from places included in the basic coverage territory.

2-5. The CGL policy stipulates that the insurer has the right and duty to defend the insured against any suit that seeks damages for bodily injury or property damage to which the insurance applies. The policy defines suit to include arbitration or other alternative dispute resolution proceedings, as well as formal lawsuits.

Educational Objective 3

3-1. Exclusion a. eliminates coverage for bodily injury or property damage that is expected or intended by the insured. However, the exclusion does not apply to bodily injury resulting from the use of reasonable force to protect persons or property. An act of protecting property would be covered despite the intentional use of force.

3-2. The CGL policy's Pollution exclusion is worded broadly to encompass the many ways pollutants can enter the environment.

3-3. The Mobile Equipment exclusion eliminates coverage for these general categories of loss:

- The transportation of mobile equipment by an auto that is owned, operated, rented, or borrowed by an insured

- The use of mobile equipment in a prearranged racing, speed, or demolition contest or in a stunting activity

3-4. The CGL policy's Damage to Property exclusion eliminates coverage for damage to any of these:

- Property owned, rented, or occupied by the named insured

- Premises the named insured has sold, given away, or abandoned if the damage arises out of any part of such premises

- Property loaned to the named insured

- Personal property in the care, custody, or control of an insured

- That particular part of any real property on which work is being done by the named insured or any contractor or subcontractor working for the named insured if the damage arises from the work

- That particular part of any property that must be restored, repaired, or replaced because the named insured's work was incorrectly performed on it

3-5. The exclusions related to the insured's products and work prevent the insurer from having to pay for failures of the insured's products or work—other than bodily injury or damage to property that is not the insured's own product or work.

Educational Objective 4

4-1. Examples of the offenses that the CGL coverage form defines as personal and advertising injury include these:

- False arrest, detention, or imprisonment

- Malicious prosecution

- Wrongful eviction from, wrongful entry into, or invasion of the right of private occupancy of a room, dwelling, or premises that a person occupies, committed by or on behalf of its owner, landlord, or lessor

- Oral or written publication, in any manner, of material that slanders or libels a person or organization or disparages a person's or organization's goods, products, or services

- Oral or written publication, in any manner, of material that violates a person's right of privacy

- The use of another's advertising idea in an advertisement

- Infringement on another's copyright, trade dress, or slogan in an advertisement

4-2. If an insured knowingly uses a competitor's advertising ideas in his or her own advertisements, the Knowing Violation of Rights of Another exclusion would apply.

4-3. The CGL policy's Contractual Liability exclusion applies to injury for which the insured has assumed liability in a contract or an agreement except for liability that the insured would have in the absence of the contract.

4-4. The CGL policy exclusion that applies in this scenario is Wrong Description of Prices.

4-5. The primary difference between the CGL Coverage A and Coverage B Pollution exclusions is that the Coverage B exclusion has no exceptions.

Educational Objective 5

5-1. Under the Coverage C insuring agreement, the insurer agrees to pay medical expenses (including, by definition, funeral expenses) for bodily injury caused by an accident.

5-2. The CGL policy's medical payments coverage does not apply to bodily injury to these categories of persons:

- Any insured (other than a volunteer worker of the named insured)

- Anyone hired to do work for an insured or for a tenant of an insured

- A person injured on that part of the named insured's premises that the person normally occupies

- A person entitled to workers compensation benefits for the injury

- A person injured while taking part in any physical exercises, games, sports, or athletic contests

5-3. The medical payments coverage provided by the CGL coverage form's Coverage C is not considered liability insurance because coverage is provided regardless of whether the insured is legally liable.

Educational Objective 6

6-1. CGL Coverage A and Coverage B are the insuring agreements supplemented by the supplementary payments section.

6-2. The supplementary payments are payable in addition to the limits of insurance that apply to CGL coverage. However, the insurer's obligation to pay these supplementary payments ends as soon as the applicable limit of insurance has been exhausted in paying damages for judgments or settlements.

6-3. The CGL coverage form includes the following supplementary payments:

- All expenses incurred by the insurer (fees for attorneys, witness fees, and cost of police reports).

- Up to $250 for the cost of bail bonds required because of accidents or traffic law violations involving any covered vehicle (typically mobile equipment).

- The cost of bonds to release any property of the insured's held by a plaintiff to ensure payment of any judgment that may be rendered against the insured. The insurer is not required to provide either of the bonds previously described; its only obligation is to pay the premium.

- Reasonable expenses incurred by the insured at the insurer's request including loss of earnings for missing work to testify, attend court, or assist in the defense.

- Court costs or other costs (excluding actual damages) assessed against the insured in a suit.

- Interest on judgments awarded against the insured.

6-4. Supplementary payments coverage will pay reasonable expenses incurred by Amelia at the insurer's request, including loss of earnings (up to $250 a day) when she must miss work to testify, attend court, or otherwise assist in the defense.

Direct Your Learning

Commercial General Liability Insurance, Part II

Educational Objectives

After learning the content of this assignment, you should be able to:

1. Determine whether a described person or organization is an insured under the Commercial General Liability Coverage Form.

2. Explain how the following limits of insurance in the Commercial General Liability (CGL) Coverage Form are applied:

   - Each occurrence limit

   - Personal and advertising injury limit

   - Damage to premises rented to you limit

   - Medical expense limit

   - General aggregate limit

   - Products-completed operations aggregate limit

3. Apply the Commercial General Liability Conditions to claims or other interactions between the insurer and the insured.

4. Explain how the premium for CGL coverage is determined.

5. Given a case, determine whether, and for what amount, the Commercial General Liability Coverage Form (occurrence version) covers a described claim.

Outline

▶ **CGL Who Is an Insured Provisions**

   A. Named Insured and Related Parties

   B. Named Insured's Employees and Volunteer Workers

   C. Other Persons and Organizations

      1. Real Estate Managers

      2. Legal Representatives

      3. Newly Acquired Organizations

   D. Unlisted Partnership, Joint Venture, or LLC—Excluded

▶ **CGL Limits of Insurance**

   A. Limits and Sublimits

   B. Applying the Limits

▶ **CGL Conditions**

   A. Bankruptcy

   B. Duties in the Event of Occurrence, Offense, Claim or Suit

   C. Legal Action Against Us

   D. Other Insurance

      1. When CGL Is Primary

      2. When CGL Is Excess

      3. Methods of Sharing

   E. Premium Audit

   F. Representations

   G. Separation of Insureds

   H. Transfer of Rights of Recovery Against Others to Us

   I. When We Do Not Renew

▶ **Rating CGL Coverage**

   A. CGL Rating Formula

   B. CGL Rates for Business Classifications

   C. Premium Base

   D. Other Rating Considerations

▶ **Determining Whether the CGL Covers a Claims Case**

   A. Case Facts

   B. Necessary Reference Materials

   C. Overview of Steps

   D. Determination of Coverage

      1. DICE Analysis Step 1: Declarations

      2. DICE Analysis Step 2: Insuring Agreement

      3. DICE Analysis Step 3: Conditions

      4. DICE Analysis Step 4: Exclusions

   E. Determination of Amounts Payable

Plan to register with The Institutes well in advance of your exam. For complete information regarding exam dates and fees, please visit our web page, www.TheInstitutes.org/forms, where you can access and print exam registration information.

For each assignment, you should define or describe each of the Key Words and Phrases and answer each of the Review and Application Questions.

Educational Objective 1

Determine whether a described person or organization is an insured under the Commercial General Liability Coverage Form.

Review Questions

1-1. Identify the persons who are automatically included as insureds if the named insured in the commercial general liability (CGL) declarations is one of these parties:

 a. An individual

 b. A partnership or joint venture

 c. A limited liability company (LLC)

d. A corporation, municipality, or school district

e. A trust

1-2. Identify persons or organizations, other than the named insured, who are insureds under the CGL.

1-3. Explain how the CGL applies to the conduct of partnerships, joint ventures, and LLCs not shown as named insureds in the policy declarations and why this is potentially problematic.

▶▶

Educational Objective 2

Explain how the following limits of insurance in the Commercial General Liability (CGL) Coverage Form are applied:

- Each occurrence limit
- Personal and advertising injury limit
- Damage to premises rented to you limit
- Medical expense limit
- General aggregate limit
- Products-completed operations aggregate limit

Key Word or Phrase

Aggregate limit

Review Questions

2-1.   Explain how the each occurrence limit in the commercial general liability (CGL) form determines the amount an insurer will pay.

2-2.   Explain the two sublimits that are subject to the CGL each occurrence limit.

2-3. Explain the CGL limit for personal and advertising injury.

2-4. Explain the purpose of the CGL aggregate limits.

2-5. Explain the CGL general aggregate limit.

2-6. Explain the CGL products-completed operations aggregate limit.

Application Question

2-7. The Sausage Company is a small business that makes various types of sausage and operates a restaurant. The company has a CGL with these limits:

General aggregate limit: $2,000,000

Products-completed operations aggregate limit: $2,000,000

Each occurrence limit: $1,000,000

Personal and advertising injury limit: $1,000,000

Damage to premises rented to you limit: $100,000

Medical expense limit: $5,000

The company owns the building where the sausage is made but leases the premises for the restaurant in a strip mall. One evening, the cook at the restaurant accidentally caused a fire. There was $110,000 damage to the restaurant building. Two customers were injured while exiting the restaurant, and the injuries resulted in damages of $325,000. No prior losses have occurred during this policy period.

a. Explain which limits apply to this loss and how much the insurer will pay.

b. During the same policy period, the restaurant used a generator to supply electricity during a power outage. Failure to operate the generator properly resulted in a release of carbon monoxide into the restaurant. Several patrons became ill. The damages for all of the patrons total $1.1 million. Explain which limits apply to this loss and how much the insurer will pay.

c. The restaurant bottles and sells jars of its famous Louisiana Sausage Jambalaya sauce. Two dozen of the jars, improperly sealed, became contaminated with botulinus toxin. During the same policy period, two customers purchased jars of the sauce and became ill with botulism before the restaurant became aware of the problem. One of these customers died. The damages were $1 million. Explain which limits apply to this loss and how much the insurer will pay.

Educational Objective 3

Apply the Commercial General Liability Conditions to claims or other interactions between the insurer and the insured.

Review Questions

3-1. What are the insured's duties in the event of an occurrence, a claim, or a suit under the Commercial General Liability (CGL) Coverage Form?

3-2. According to the CGL conditions, under what circumstances can the insured bring legal action against the insurer?

3-3. Explain how loss payment under two or more CGL policies would be shared using these methods:

   a.   Contribution by equal shares

b. Contribution by limits

3-4. Summarize each of these CGL conditions:

a. Premium Audit

b. Representations

c. Separation of Insureds

d. Transfer of Right of Recovery Against Others

Application Question

3-5.   A manufacturing company is insured under two CGL policies. The each occurrence limit under Policy A is $500,000. Under Policy B, the each occurrence limit is $1,000,000. The company was held to be legally liable for $300,000 in damages arising from one occurrence.

   a.   What dollar amount would be payable under each policy if loss payment is based on contribution by limits? Show your calculations.

   b.   What dollar amount would be payable under each policy if loss payment is based on contribution by equal shares?

Educational Objective 4

Explain how the premium for CGL coverage is determined.

Key Words and Phrases

Premium base

Class code

Review Questions

4-1. What is the formula used to determine the premium for commercial general liability (CGL) coverage?

4-2. Differentiate between rate and exposure.

4-3. Explain why two rates are used for most businesses when determining the premium for CGL coverage.

4-4. Indicate an example of a premium base that may be used in rating CGL coverage for each of these businesses or events:

   a.   Mercantile businesses

b.   Contracting businesses

c.   Special events

Educational Objective 5

Given a case, determine whether, and for what amount, the Commercial General Liability Coverage Form (occurrence version) covers a described claim.

Application Questions

5-1.   A construction company is insured under a commercial general liability (CGL) policy with a $1,000,000 general aggregate limit, a $1,000,000 products-completed operations aggregate limit, and a $500,000 each occurrence limit. The company was sued separately by two bystanders who were injured in the same accident at one of the company's construction sites. The court awarded $200,000 to the first bystander and $250,000 to the second bystander. The total cost of defending the company in these two lawsuits was $80,000. To what extent, if any, will these amounts be paid by the company's CGL insurer? Explain.

5-2. A manufacturer of small home appliances is insured under a CGL policy written on an occurrence basis with a $1,000,000 personal and advertising injury limit of insurance. The manufacturer placed an advertisement in a national magazine that made inaccurate and unfavorable statements about a competitor's product. The competitor sued the manufacturer for libel and was awarded $1,500,000 in court. What dollar amount, if any, will the manufacturer's CGL insurer pay for the loss? (Assume that the loss occurred during the policy period.)

Answers to Assignment 7 Questions

NOTE: These answers are provided to give students a basic understanding of acceptable types of responses. They often are not the only valid answers and are not intended to provide an exhaustive response to the questions.

Educational Objective 1

1-1. Individuals are automatically included as insureds if the named insured in the CGL declaration is one of these parties:

   a.   If the named insured is an individual, the named insured's spouse is also an insured.

   b.   If the named insured is a partnership or joint venture, all partners or members and their spouses are also insureds.

   c.   If the named insured is an LLC, controlling members and managers of the company are also insureds.

   d.   All executive officers, directors, and stockholders of the organization are also insureds.

   e.   If the named insured is a trust (a legal entity created for the benefit of designated beneficiaries), the named trust is an insured. The named insured's trustees are also insureds, but only with respect to their duties as trustees.

1-2. Other than the named insured, the following are insureds under the CGL:

   •   Employees and volunteer workers of the named insured

   •   Real estate managers

   •   Legal representatives

   •   Newly acquired organizations (for ninety days maximum)

1-3. Coverage does not apply to the conduct of any current or past partnership, joint venture, or LLC that is not shown as a named insured in the policy declarations. Such entities are covered only if they are specifically declared and named in the policy. The insurer will usually charge an additional premium for covering the added loss exposure.

Educational Objective 2

2-1. The each occurrence limit is the most the insurer will pay for any one occurrence, regardless of the number of persons insured, the number of claims or lawsuits brought, or the number of persons or organizations making claims, and including all damages under Coverage A and all medical payments under Coverage C. Defense costs do not apply to the each occurrence limit.

2-2. The damage to premises rented to you limit and the medical expense limit are sublimits that are subject to the Coverage A each occurrence limit.

   The damage to premises rented to you limit is the most the insurer will pay under Coverage A for damage to any one premises while rented to the named insured or, in the case of fire damage, while rented to or temporarily occupied by the named insured.

   The medical expense limit is the most the insurer will pay under Coverage C to any one person.

2-3. The personal and advertising limit is the most the insurer will pay under Coverage B for damages arising out of personal and advertising injury to any one person or organization. It is usually the same as the policy's each occurrence limit, although a different amount can be used.

2-4. The CGL aggregate limits cap the total amount of damages that the insurer will pay for the entire policy period, although defense costs do not apply.

2-5. The general aggregate limit is the most the insurer will pay for the sum of damages under Coverage A (except those that arise out of the products-completed operations hazard) and Coverage B, and medical expenses under Coverage C.

2-6. The products-completed operations aggregate limit is the most the insurer will pay under Coverage A for bodily injury or property damage included in the "products-completed operations hazard." The CGL defines this hazard to include bodily injury and property damage occurring away from premises owned or rented by the named insured and arising out of the named insured's product or work.

2-7. These answers apply to questions regarding The Sausage Company's CGL policy:

    a. The each occurrence limit of $1,000,000 applies to this loss, and all of the damages are within that limit. The $325,000 damages for the customer's injuries will be paid by the insurer. There is a $100,000 sublimit for damage to premises rented to you. The insurer will pay $100,000 for the damage to the restaurant building. The $425,000 paid by the insurer is applied to the general aggregate limit of $2,000,000, reducing it to $1,575,000.

    b. The each occurrence limit of $1,000,000 will apply to this loss, and the insurer will pay $1,000,000. The general aggregate limit will also apply, and that limit is now $575,000.

    c. The each occurrence limit applies to this loss. Additionally, the products-completed operations aggregate limit applies to this loss. The damages of $1 million are within both of these limits.

Educational Objective 3

3-1. The insured's duties in the event of an occurrence, a claim, or a suit under a CGL coverage form include these:

- Provide notice of how, when, and where the occurrence or offense happened

- Provide the name and addresses of any injured persons and any witnesses

- Describe the nature and location of any damage or injury resulting from the occurrence or offense

- Immediately record the details of the claim or suit and the date received

- Notify the insurer in writing as soon as practicable

- Immediately forward the insurer copies of any legal papers related to the suit

- Authorize the insurer to obtain any legal records or other documents

- Cooperate with the insurer in the investigation or settlement of the claim or in the insurer's defense against the suit

- Assist the insurer in any action against any third party that may be liable to the insured because of the injuries or damage for which claim is made

- Refrain from making voluntary payments, assuming obligations, or incurring any expenses without the insurer's consent

3-2. According to CGL conditions, the insured can sue the insurer to force the insurer to pay a third-party claim only if the insured has fully complied with all policy conditions.

3-3. Loss payment under two or more CGL policies would be shared in this fashion:

a. Contribution by equal shares—Each insurer contributes an equal amount to the payment of the claim until the claim is fully paid or one insurer exhausts its limit of insurance, whichever occurs first.

b. Contribution by limits—Each insurer pays that proportion of the claim that its limit bears to the total of all applicable insurance. Neither insurer will pay more than its applicable limit of insurance.

3-4. The CGL conditions are summarized in this manner:

a. The Premium Audit CGL condition requires the named insured to keep adequate records to permit correct calculation of the premium and to make these records available to the insurer.

b. The Representations CGL condition states that, by accepting the policy, the named insured agrees to the following: The statements in the declarations are accurate and complete; the statements in the declarations are based on representations made by the named insured to the insurer; and the insurer has issued the policy in reliance on the named insured's representations. This condition encourages the insured to read the policy declarations and make sure that the representations made in the policy are accurate.

c. The Separation of Insureds CGL condition states that the insurance provided by the policy applies separately to each person insured. If one insured sues another insured, coverage is provided for the insured who has been sued.

d. If the insured has any right to recover from a third party all or any part of a claim paid by the insurer, the insured must transfer that right to the insurer. The insurer is subrogated to the rights of the insured to recover the amount paid.

3-5. The answers to the questions regarding methods of sharing under the manufacturing company's CGL policies are these:

a. The dollar amounts payable under each policy if loss payment is based on contribution by limits are these:

Policy A: $500,000/$1,500,000 × $300,000 = $100,000

Policy B: $1,000,000/$1,500,000 × $300,000 = $200,000

b. If loss payment is based on contribution by equal shares, Policy A will pay $150,000 and Policy B will pay $150,000.

Educational Objective 4

4-1. The formula used to determine the premium for CGL coverage is rate times exposure equals premium.

4-2. The rate depends on the nature of the insured organization and its susceptibility to liability losses. The exposure reflects the size of business operations insured, not the type of losses to which the business is susceptible.

4-3. The premium for CGL coverage for most businesses is determined through the use of two rates because one rate applies to the exposure for premises operations, and another rate applies to the exposure for products-completed operations.

4-4. The premium bases normally used in rating CGL coverages are these:

a. The premium base used for mercantile businesses is gross sales.

b. The premium base used for contracting businesses is payroll.

c. The premium base used for special events is the number of admissions.

Educational Objective 5

5-1. The insurer will pay all the damages awarded to both bystanders because the total ($450,000) is less than the each occurrence limit. The insurer will also pay the $80,000 in defense costs in full because defense costs are payable in addition to the policy limits.

5-2. The manufacturer's CGL insurer will pay $1,000,000—the personal and advertising injury limit.

Direct Your Learning

Commercial Auto Insurance

Educational Objectives

After learning the content of this assignment, you should be able to:

1. Describe commercial auto insurance in terms of these elements:
    - The loss exposures that can be covered
    - The components of a commercial auto coverage part

2. Select the symbols needed to provide a described organization with appropriate commercial auto coverage(s) under the Business Auto Coverage Form.

3. Summarize the provisions contained in Section II—Covered Autos Liability Coverage of the Business Auto Coverage Form.

4. Summarize the provisions contained in Section III—Physical Damage of the Business Auto Coverage Form.

5. Describe the conditions contained in the Business Auto Coverage Form.

6. Describe the following coverages that may be added by endorsement to the Business Auto Coverage Form:
    - Medical payments
    - Personal injury protection and added personal injury protection
    - Uninsured and underinsured motorists

7. Explain how the following are rated for commercial auto coverage:
    - Private passenger vehicles
    - Trucks, tractors, and trailers

8. Given a case, determine whether, and for what amount, the Business Auto Coverage Form covers a described claim.

Outline

▶ **Overview of Commercial Auto Insurance**

  A. Commercial Auto Loss Exposures

    1. Liability Loss Exposures

    2. Property Loss Exposures

    3. Personal Loss Exposures

  B. Components of a Commercial Auto Coverage Part

    1. Declarations

    2. Coverage Forms

    3. Endorsements

▶ **BACF Covered Autos**

  A. How Coverage Symbols Work

  B. Defining the Term "Auto"

  C. BACF's Auto Coverage Symbols

  D. Symbols 1 and 19 Explained

  E. Coverage for Newly Acquired Autos

  F. Other Covered Items

▶ **BACF Covered Autos Liability Coverage**

  A. Insuring Agreement

    1. Duty to Pay Damages

    2. Duty to Pay "Covered Pollution Cost or Expense"

    3. Duty to Defend

  B. Who Is an Insured

  C. Person Held Liable for the Conduct of an Insured

  D. Coverage Extensions

  E. Exclusions

    1. Expected or Intended Injury and Contractual Liability Exclusions

    2. Workers Compensation and Related Exclusions

    3. Care, Custody, or Control Exclusion

    4. Exclusions Related to Loading and Unloading

    5. Operations and Completed Operations Exclusions

    6. Pollution, War, and Racing Exclusions

  F. Limit of Insurance

▶ **BACF Physical Damage Coverage**

  A. Available Coverages

    1. Collision Coverage

    2. Comprehensive Coverage

    3. Specified Causes of Loss Coverage

    4. Towing Coverage

    5. Transportation Expenses

    6. Loss of Use Expenses

  B. Exclusions

  C. Limit of Insurance

  D. Deductible

▶ **Business Auto Coverage Form Conditions**

  A. Loss Conditions

    1. Appraisal for Physical Damage Losses

    2. Duties in the Event of an Accident, Claim, Suit or Loss

    3. Legal Action Against the Insurer

    4. Loss Payment—Physical Damage Coverages

    5. Transfer of Rights Against Others

  B. General Conditions

    1. Bankruptcy

    2. Concealment, Misrepresentation, or Fraud

    3. Liberalization

    4. No Benefit to Bailee—Physical Damage Insurance Only

    5. Other Insurance

    6. Premium Audit

    7. Policy Period, Coverage Territory

    8. Two or More Coverage Forms or Policies Issued by the Insurer

▶ **Business Auto Coverages Added by Endorsement**

  A. Medical Payments

  B. Personal Injury Protection and Added Personal Injury Protection

  C. Uninsured and Underinsured Motorists Insurance

    1. Uninsured Motorists (UM) Coverage

    2. Underinsured Motorists (UIM) Coverage

▶ **Rating Commercial Auto Insurance**

  A. Private Passenger Vehicles

  B. Trucks, Tractors, and Trailers

    1. Primary Factor

    2. Premium Computation

Before starting a new assignment, briefly review the Educational Objectives of those preceding it.

Outline

▶ **Determining Whether the BACF Covers a Claim**

   A. Case Facts

   B. Necessary Reference Materials

   C. Overview of Steps

   D. Determination of Coverage

      1. DICE Analysis Step 1: Declarations

      2. DICE Analysis Step 2: Insuring Agreement

      3. DICE Analysis Step 3: Conditions

      4. DICE Analysis Step 4: Exclusions

      5. Coverage Extensions

   E. Determination of Amounts Payable

For each assignment, you should define or describe each of the Key Words and Phrases and answer each of the Review and Application Questions.

Educational Objective 1

Describe commercial auto insurance in terms of these elements:

- **The loss exposures that can be covered**
- **The components of a commercial auto coverage part**

Key Words and Phrases

Employers nonownership liability

Garagekeepers coverage

Review Questions

1-1. Identify the three basic categories of commercial auto loss exposures.

1-2. Identify the most common way a business can incur auto liability.

1-3.   Identify situations in which an organization can become liable for injury or damage to others that results from the use of autos it does not own.

1-4.   Identify the purpose of garagekeepers coverage.

1-5.   Describe the main consequences of damage to or destruction of an auto from the perspective of the auto's owner.

1-6.   Describe the various commercial auto coverages that cover personal loss exposures arising from auto accidents.

1-7. Identify what types of insureds are eligible for the Business Auto Coverage Form.

1-8. Describe the purposes for adding endorsements to commercial auto coverage forms.

Educational Objective 2

Select the symbols needed to provide a described organization with appropriate commercial auto coverage(s) under the Business Auto Coverage Form.

Review Questions

2-1. Explain the numerical symbol system used to indicate the covered autos for the various coverages available under the Business Auto Coverage Form (BACF).

2-2. Identify the ten symbols the BACF uses to signify coverage.

2-3. Contrast the coverage for newly acquired autos provided by symbols 1 through 6 or 19 with that provided by symbol 7 in the BACF.

2-4. Identify the main situation in which symbol 19 is useful.

Application Question

2-5. Howard is a local beverage distributor who owns four delivery trucks. In ordinary circumstances, these four vehicles handle all of his business needs. On occasion, when one vehicle is out of service, Howard's employees will use their own cars to make small deliveries. For liability coverage in his Business Auto Coverage Form, what symbol or symbols are appropriate for Howard's business?

Educational Objective 3

Summarize the provisions contained in Section II—Covered Autos Liability Coverage of the Business Auto Coverage Form.

Review Questions

3-1. Identify the three distinct duties that an insurer has under the Business Auto Coverage Form (BACF) liability coverage agreement.

3-2. What determines whether a vehicle qualifies as a covered auto under the BACF?

3-3. Identify the circumstances under which the BACF will cover pollution cost or expense.

3-4. Describe who is an insured under the BACF.

▶▶

3-5. Identify the six supplementary payments BACF liability coverage provides.

3-6. Identify the categories of exclusions in the BACF.

Educational Objective 4

Summarize the provisions contained in Section III—Physical Damage of the Business Auto Coverage Form.

Review Questions

4-1. Identify the three basic physical damage coverages from which the insured may choose under the Business Auto Coverage Form (BACF).

4-2. Explain what is included in the BACF's Collision Coverage.

4-3. Explain what is included in the BACF's Comprehensive Coverage.

4-4. Identify examples of perils insured under the BACF's Specified Causes of Loss Coverage.

4-5. Identify examples of the types of electronic equipment excluded under the BACF.

4-6. Describe the BACF's determination of the most the insurer will pay for a physical damage loss.

Educational Objective 5
Describe the conditions contained in the Business Auto Coverage Form.

Review Questions

5-1. Describe the insured's duties after a loss.

5-2. Describe the insurer's loss payment options with regard to damaged or stolen property under the Business Auto Coverage Form.

5-3. Describe the insurer's right known as subrogation.

Application Question

5-4. Hector runs a cheese shop in a large city. One of his trucks is involved in a liability claim, and two primary business auto policies apply to the claim. Policy A has a $300,000 liability limit, and Policy B has a $500,000 liability limit. The covered amount of the claim is determined to be $160,000. Using the Other Insurance provision of the business auto conditions, how much coverage, if any, is provided to Hector by Policy A and by Policy B?

Educational Objective 6

Describe the following coverages that may be added by endorsement to the Business Auto Coverage Form:

- **Medical payments**
- **Personal injury protection and added personal injury protection**
- **Uninsured and underinsured motorists**

Review Questions

6-1. Describe the coverage provided by the auto medical payments insurance available by endorsement to the Business Auto Coverage Form (BACF).

6-2. Identify the persons covered by auto medical payments insurance in the BACF.

6-3. Describe the benefits provided by a typical personal injury protection (PIP) endorsement to a BACF.

6-4. Describe the coverage provided by uninsured motorists insurance in the BACF.

Application Question

6-5. Lorena owns an electrical repair service and insures her service vehicles under the BACF. She lives and works in a state that has enacted a no-fault law. Her business auto policy includes liability, PIP, uninsured motorists (UM) ($300,000 limit), and underinsured motorists (UIM) ($300,000 limit) coverages. She is injured in an accident involving the service truck she was driving. In court, the other party is found to be 100 percent responsible for the accident, and Lorena is awarded $100,000 for her pain and suffering. The negligent party carried auto liability limits of $25,000. Lorena also incurs $150,000 of medical expenses. What coverage, if any, from Lorena's business auto policy will apply?

Educational Objective 7

Explain how the following are rated for commercial auto coverage:

- **Private passenger vehicles**
- **Trucks, tractors, and trailers**

Key Word or Phrase

Zone rated vehicles

Review Questions

7-1. Identify the three components of the primary factor used in rating trucks, tractors, and trailers for business auto insurance.

7-2. Explain how base liability premiums and base physical damage coverage premiums are determined for non-zone rated vehicles.

7-3. Explain how base premiums and base physical damage premiums are determined for zone rated vehicles.

Application Question

7-4. Worthley Grocery has a small chain of grocery stores in five states. It maintains six trucks and trailers to purchase organic produce from wholesalers and carry the produce to its stores. Worthley entered into agreements with other organic grocers with whom it shares the produce distribution within a five-state area so that its trucks and trailers were only transporting produce in a 175-mile radius. However, due to the demand for fresh produce in the winter, Worthley is regularly sending some trucks with trailers 700 miles to warmer states for produce. Explain how Worthley's insurer will determine the rates for the vehicles that are now traveling the longer distances.

Educational Objective 8

Given a case, determine whether, and for what amount, the Business Auto Coverage Form covers a described claim.

Application Question

8-1. CPS, a supplier of commercial printing equipment, is insured under a commercial package policy that includes the Business Auto Coverage Form (BACF). No endorsements that would modify the BACF are attached to the policy.

The Business Auto Declarations in CPS's policy show the policy period as running from July 1, 20X0, to July 1, 20X1. The Schedule of Coverages and Covered Autos indicates covered auto symbol 1 and a $1 million limit of insurance for BACF liability coverage.

On November 1, 20X0, Malamute Publishing (MP) paid $100,000 to purchase a commercial-grade printer from CPS, which agreed to deliver the printer 150 miles to MP's premises (in the United States). On November 3, CPS assigned Josh, a CPS employee, to deliver the printer to MP's premises in a CPS truck. While driving to MP's premises, Josh fell asleep at the wheel, causing the truck to collide with another auto, driven by Rhonda. Both vehicles and MP's printer were destroyed, and both Josh and Rhonda were severely injured.

Josh's medical expenses and income loss were covered by workers compensation. However, Rhonda and MP made these liability claims against CPS, for which CPS sought coverage under its BACF:

Claim 1: Rhonda made a claim against CPS for $900,000 in damages for her bodily injury and another $20,000 in damages for property damage to her auto. Her claim alleged that her damages resulted from Josh's negligent operation of CPS's truck and that CPS was legally liable for the damages as Josh's employer.

Claim 2: MP made a claim against CPS for $100,000 in damages for destruction of the printer. The claim alleged that the printer (which MP owned at the time of the loss) was damaged as a result of Josh's negligent operation of CPS's truck and that CPS was legally liable for the damages as Josh's employer.

After investigating both claims, CPS's insurer concluded that CPS was legally liable for the full amount of damages alleged in each claim.

a. Disregarding the requirement that the insurance must apply to the bodily injury or property damage, do Claim 1 and Claim 2 meet the other conditions imposed by the insuring agreement in Section II—Covered Autos Liability Coverage of the BACF? Explain why or why not.

b. Assuming that none of the conditions in Section IV—Business Auto Conditions would eliminate coverage for Claim 1, do any of the exclusions in Section II—Covered Autos Liability Coverage eliminate coverage for Claim 1? If so, identify any exclusion(s) that would eliminate coverage, and explain why each exclusion would apply.

c.   Assuming that none of the conditions in Section IV—Business Auto
     Conditions would eliminate coverage for Claim 2, do any of the exclusions
     in Section II—Covered Autos Liability Coverage eliminate coverage for
     Claim 2? If so, identify any exclusion(s) that would eliminate coverage,
     and explain why each exclusion would apply.

d.   What is the total amount of damages payable by CPS's insurer for both
     Claim 1 and Claim 2?

Answers to Assignment 8 Questions

NOTE: These answers are provided to give students a basic understanding of acceptable types of responses. They often are not the only valid answers and are not intended to provide an exhaustive response to the questions.

Educational Objective 1

1-1.   The three basic categories of commercial auto loss exposures are liability loss exposures, property loss exposures, and personal loss exposures.

1-2.   The most common way a business can incur auto liability is through the negligent injury of persons or damage to property by an employee operating an auto owned by the business.

1-3.   In several situations, an organization can become liable for injury or damage to others that results from the use of autos it does not own. An employee may use his or her own auto to further an employer's business. Another example is when an organization hires autos from other organizations for terms ranging from a few hours to a number of years. Whatever the period of time, the hiring organization can be held legally liable for injury that results from the vehicle's operation. Similarly, a person or an organization that borrows an auto from another can be held liable for injury arising from its operation.

1-4.   The purpose of garagekeepers coverage is to insure loss to customers' autos while they are in the custody of the insured auto or trailer dealer.

1-5.   The main consequences of the damage to or destruction of an auto are a decrease in or loss of the auto's value and loss of use of the auto until it can be repaired or replaced.

1-6.   Auto medical payments coverage, personal injury protection coverage, and uninsured motorists coverage cover personal loss exposures arising from auto accidents.

1-7.   Any organizations other than auto or trailer dealers and motor carriers (businesses that transport the property of others) are eligible for the Business Auto Coverage Form.

1-8.   Endorsements are commonly used to add coverages, to designate additional insureds, to add or omit exclusions, and to bring standard coverage forms into conformity with state insurance regulations.

Educational Objective 2

2-1.   The Business Auto Coverage Form uses numerical symbols to indicate covered autos. One or more of these numerical symbols are entered beside each coverage listed in the policy schedule to indicate which types of autos are covered.

2-2. The ten symbols the BACF uses to signify coverage are these:

- Symbol 1—Any Auto

- Symbol 2—Owned Autos Only

- Symbol 3—Owned Private Passenger Autos Only

- Symbol 4—Owned Autos Other Than Private Passenger Autos Only

- Symbol 5—Owned Autos Subject to No-Fault

- Symbol 6—Owned Autos Subject to a Compulsory Uninsured Motorists Law

- Symbol 7—Specifically Described Autos

- Symbol 8—Hired Autos Only

- Symbol 9—Nonowned Autos Only

- Symbol 19—Mobile Equipment Subject to Compulsory or Financial Responsibility or Other Motor Vehicle Insurance Law Only

2-3. If symbols 1 through 6 or 19 are used, newly acquired autos of the type indicated by the symbol are automatically covered. The insurer will learn of newly acquired autos at the end of the policy period (during the audit), and the insured will pay the additional premium. If symbol 7 is used, newly acquired autos are covered from the time of acquisition only if the insurer insures all autos owned by the named insured, or the newly acquired auto replaces a covered auto and the named insured asks the insurer to cover the newly acquired auto within thirty days after the acquisition.

2-4. The main situation in which symbol 19 is useful is when an insured has coverage through symbol 7 (specifically described autos).

2-5. Howard will have coverage for any auto, owned or nonowned, if symbol 1 is entered for liability coverage. Because vehicles used in the business are limited to owned vehicles and those of his employees, he can alternatively use symbols 2 and 9.

Educational Objective 3

3-1. In the liability coverage agreement, the insurer expresses three distinct duties:

- A duty to pay damages

- A duty to pay "covered pollution cost or expense"

- A duty to defend the insured

3-2. Whether a vehicle qualifies as a covered auto depends on what coverage symbols are indicated in the schedule of coverages and what covered autos are listed in the business auto declarations.

3-3. For pollution cost or expense to be covered, under the BACF, it must be caused by an accident and must result from the ownership, maintenance, or use of a covered auto. In addition, the same accident that causes the pollution cost or expense must also result in bodily injury or property damage covered by the policy.

3-4. The named insured is an insured for any covered auto. Anyone other than the named insured is an insured while using with the named insured's permission a covered auto owned, hired, or borrowed by the named insured, subject to certain restrictions.

3-5. BACF liability coverage provides six supplementary payments, which are payable in addition to the limit of insurance:

- All expenses incurred by the insurer

- Up to $2,000 for the cost of bail bonds required because of a covered accident

- The cost of bonds to release attachments in any suit against the insured that the insurer defends

- All reasonable expenses incurred by the insured at the insurer's request

- All court costs taxed against the insured in any suit against the insured defended by the insurer

- All interest on the full amount of any judgment that accrues after entry of the judgment in any suit against the insured that the insurer defends

3-6. The exclusions that appear in the BACF's liability coverage section impose several limitations on the liability insuring agreement:

- Expected or intended injury and contractual liability exclusions

- Workers compensation and related exclusions

- Care, custody, or control exclusion

- Exclusions related to loading and unloading

- Operations and completed operations exclusions

- Pollution, war, and racing exclusions

Educational Objective 4

4-1. Under the BACF, the insured may choose from three basic physical damage coverages:

- Collision Coverage

- Comprehensive Coverage

- Specified Causes of Loss Coverage

4-2. The BACF's Collision Coverage insures direct and accidental loss or damage to a covered auto caused by collision with another object or by overturn.

4-3. The BACF's Comprehensive Coverage insures direct and accidental loss or damage to a covered auto by any peril except collision or overturn or a peril specifically excluded.

4-4. Examples of perils insured under the BACF's Specified Causes of Loss Coverage include direct and accidental loss caused by fire, lightning, explosion, theft, windstorm, hail, earthquake, flood, mischief, vandalism, or loss resulting from the sinking, burning, collision, or derailment of a conveyance transporting the covered auto.

4-5. The BACF excludes many, but not all, types of electronic equipment in a covered auto. The insurer will not pay for loss to these items:

- Tapes, records, discs, or similar devices

- Radar detectors, laser detectors, and similar devices

- Any equipment, regardless of whether it is permanently installed, that reproduces, receives, or transmits audio, visual, or data signals

- Any accessories used with the previously described equipment

4-6. The most the insurer will pay for a physical damage loss is the lesser of these values:

- The actual cash value of the property at the time of loss

- The cost of repairing or replacing the property with other property of like kind or quality

Educational Objective 5

5-1. The insured's duties after a loss are essentially the same as those imposed by the commercial general liability (CGL) policy. The named insured must give prompt notice of accident or loss to the insurer or its agent and assist the insurer in obtaining the names of injured persons or witnesses. Also, both the named insured and any other person who seeks liability coverage under the policy (for example, the driver of an insured vehicle) must do these:

- Cooperate with the insurer in its investigation and defense of the accident or loss

- Immediately send to the insurer copies of any notices or legal papers received in connection with the accident or loss

- Submit to physical examinations by physicians selected and paid by the insurer as often as the insurer may reasonably request

- Authorize the insurer to obtain medical reports and other medical information

5-2. The insurer has the following loss payment options for damaged or stolen property under the Business Auto Coverage Form:

- Pay to repair or replace the property

- Return the property at the expense of the insurer and repair any damage caused by theft

- Keep all of the property and pay an agreed or appraised value

5-3. Subrogation entails the insured's right to recover a loss from some other party, usually because the other party caused the loss. If the insurer pays the loss, it is entitled, under this condition, to take over the insured's right of recovery from the other party.

5-4. Policy A, which has three-eighths of the total limits ($300,000/$800,000), would pay $60,000 ($160,000 × 3/8), and Policy B, which has five-eighths of the total limits ($500,000/$800,000), would pay $100,000 ($160,000 × 5/8).

Educational Objective 6

6-1. The coverage provided by the auto medical payments insurance available by endorsement to the BACF is for reasonable and necessary medical and funeral expenses incurred by a person injured by an auto accident. The coverage applies regardless of fault.

6-2. The persons covered by auto medical payments insurance in the BACF are persons injured by an accident while "occupying" (entering into, riding in, or alighting from) a covered auto. If the named insured is an individual, the named insured and members of his or her family are covered while occupying any auto or if struck by an auto while a pedestrian.

6-3. The benefits provided by a typical PIP endorsement are payable for expenses resulting from bodily injury to occupants of a covered auto because of an auto accident, and they consist of the following:

- Medical and rehabilitation expenses
- Income loss benefit
- Substitute services benefit
- Death benefits to survivors

6-4. Uninsured motorists insurance covers any person injured by a legally liable uninsured motorist while riding in an auto insured under the policy. Benefits are paid to the injured person by his or her own insurer.

6-5. Lorena's PIP coverage pays medical benefits regardless of fault. Hence, Lorena's business auto policy will pay her medical expenses (subject to her PIP limit). Lorena's UIM coverage can be applied to all damages resulting from bodily injury in an auto accident (including medical expenses that may exceed her PIP limit). Unlike PIP coverage, Lorena may find compensation under UIM for her noneconomic losses (pain and suffering) related to injuries sustained in the auto accident. The UIM coverage will pay the $75,000 portion of her pain and suffering award (the amount that exceeds the $25,000 provided by the negligent party's insurer).

Educational Objective 7

7-1. The three components of the primary factor for rating business auto insurance are size, class, business use, and radius class.

7-2. The base premiums for liability and physical damage coverage for non-zone rated vehicles are multiplied by the combined factors (sum of primary and secondary factors). Base liability premiums are determined on the basis of the policy limit and the territory in which the auto is principally garaged. Base physical damage premiums are determined on the basis of the vehicle's age and its cost new.

7-3. After the primary factor has been determined for the zone rated vehicle, its physical damage and liability premiums are calculated by applying the primary factor to base premiums. Secondary factors are not used for zone rated autos.

Base premiums for zone rated vehicles are affected by the various geographical zones in which the vehicles are operated because liability and collision losses are more likely in metropolitan areas than on the open road. Base physical damage premiums depend on the vehicle's cost new, the current age of the vehicle, the type of vehicle (with respect to collision coverage), and the chosen deductible.

7-4. The trucks and trailers that are now traveling a 700-mile radius will be zone rated. The primary rating factors will not change. However, the zone rating for these vehicles, which will apply to the collision and liability premiums, will be based on the geographical zones in which the vehicles are operated.

Educational Objective 8

8-1. These answers apply to the CPS case:

   a. Yes. CPS, the named insured, qualifies as an insured for this accident because CPS is an insured for any covered auto. CPS was legally liable for the alleged damages, as determined by the insurer. The damages claimed by both Rhonda and MP resulted from bodily injury and property damage. The bodily injury and property damage were caused by an accident and resulted from the ownership, maintenance, or use of a covered auto (because CPS has symbol 1 for liability coverage).

   b. None of the exclusions eliminate coverage for Claim 1.

   c. The Care, Custody, or Control exclusion eliminates coverage for Claim 2 because MP's claim sought reimbursement for the property damage to its printer, which occurred while the printer was being transported by CPS and in CPS's care, custody, or control.

   d. CPS's insurer will pay $920,000 in damages for Claim 1 because the amount of Rhonda's damages is less than the $1 million limit for liability coverage under CPS's BACF. The insurer will not pay anything for Claim 2 because this claim is excluded.

Direct Your Learning

Workers Compensation and Employers Liability Insurance

Educational Objectives

After learning the content of this assignment, you should be able to:

1. Describe workers compensation statutes in terms of these common characteristics:

   - Basic purpose

   - Benefits provided

   - Persons and employments covered

2. Describe workers compensation statutes in terms of these common characteristics:

   - Extraterritorial provisions

   - Federal jurisdiction

   - Methods for meeting employers' obligations

3. Summarize these sections of the Workers Compensation and Employers Liability Insurance Policy:

   - Information Page

   - General Section

   - Part One—Workers Compensation Insurance

4. Explain why employers liability insurance is needed and how the Workers Compensation and Employers Liability Insurance Policy addresses this need.

5. Describe the purpose and operation of Part Three—Other States Insurance in the Workers Compensation and Employers Liability Insurance Policy.

9

Educational Objectives, continued

6. Describe the need for and the coverage provided by each of the following endorsements:

    - Voluntary Compensation and Employers' Liability Coverage Endorsement

    - Longshore and Harbor Workers' Compensation Act Coverage Endorsement

7. Explain how premium bases, classifications, and premium adjustments affect the rating of workers compensation insurance.

8. Given a case, determine whether the Workers Compensation and Employers Liability Insurance Policy covers a described injury or illness and, if so, what types of benefits or what amount of damages is covered.

Outline

▸ **Workers Compensation Statutes: Purpose, Benefits, and Persons Covered**
  A. Basic Purpose
  B. Benefits Provided
     1. Medical Benefits
     2. Disability Income Benefits
     3. Rehabilitation Benefits
     4. Death Benefits
  C. Persons and Employments Covered
     1. Employees and Independent Contractors
     2. Leased Employees and Temporary Employees

▸ **Workers Compensation Statutes: Extraterritorial Provisions, Federal Jurisdiction, and Methods for Meeting Employers' Obligations**
  A. Extraterritorial Provisions
     1. Application of Laws Out of State
     2. Application of Laws in Foreign Countries
  B. Federal Jurisdiction
  C. Methods for Meeting Employers' Obligations
     1. Voluntary Insurance
     2. Assigned Risk Plans
     3. State Funds and Employers Mutual Insurance Companies
     4. Qualified Self-Insurance Plans
     5. Self-Insured Groups

▸ **WC&EL Policy—Workers Compensation Insurance**
  A. Information Page
  B. General Section
  C. Part One—Workers Compensation Insurance

▸ **WC&EL Policy—Employers Liability Insurance**
  A. Employers Liability Insuring Agreement
  B. Employers Liability Exclusions
     1. Statutory Obligations
     2. Injury Outside the United States or Canada
     3. Liability Assumed Under Contract
     4. Employment Practices
     5. Other Exclusions
  C. Limits of Liability

▸ **WC&EL Policy—Other States Insurance**

▸ **Workers Compensation and Employers Liability Insurance Policy—Endorsements**
  A. Voluntary Compensation and Employers Liability Coverage Endorsement
  B. LHWCA Coverage Endorsement

▸ **Rating Workers Compensation Insurance**
  A. Classifications
  B. Premium Base
  C. Audits
  D. Premium Adjustments
     1. Experience Rating
     2. Retrospective Rating
     3. Premium Discount
     4. Merit or Schedule Rating Factors
     5. Rate Deviations
     6. Expense Constant
     7. Deductible Plans
     8. Dividend Plans

▸ **Determining Whether the WC&EL Policy Covers a Claim**
  A. Case Facts
  B. Necessary Reference Materials
  C. Overview of Steps
  D. Determination of Coverage
     1. DICE Analysis Step 1: Declarations
     2. DICE Analysis Step 2: Insuring Agreement
     3. DICE Analysis Step 3: Conditions
     4. DICE Analysis Step 4: Exclusions
  E. Determination of Amounts Payable

 Reward yourself after you reach specific goals.

For each assignment, you should define or describe each of the Key Words and Phrases and answer each of the Review and Application Questions.

Educational Objective 1

Describe workers compensation statutes in terms of these common characteristics:

- **Basic purpose**
- **Benefits provided**
- **Persons and employments covered**

Key Words and Phrases

Workers compensation statute

Occupational disease

Temporary partial disability (TPD)

Temporary total disability (TTD)

Employee

Independent contractor

Review Questions

1-1. Explain the basic requirements for an injury or a disease to be covered for workers compensation benefits.

1-2. Briefly explain the types of benefits included under these categories:

a. Medical benefits

b. Disability income benefits

c. Rehabilitation benefits

d. Death benefits

1-3. Identify the employees and the types of employment that are frequently excluded from state workers compensation statutes.

1-4. Why is it important for a principal to verify that its independent contractors carry valid workers compensation insurance on their employees?

Application Questions

1-5. Fran was attending a training class on behalf of her employer at a professional training center in a bordering state. She had rented a car to get to and from her hotel room and the training center. While driving to the training class, she was rear ended. She suffered injuries requiring medical care and incurred lost wages (as she was unable to work for several weeks). What benefits are payable to Fran under her employer's workers compensation coverage?

1-6. Steve was employed by a temporary employment agency and was assigned to a department store during the Christmas shopping season. While lifting a heavy box, he strained his back and then required medical care and rehabilitation. He also incurred a month of lost wages. Which employer's workers compensation policy, if any, will provide benefits for Steve's injury?

Educational Objective 2

Describe workers compensation statutes in terms of these common characteristics:

- **Extraterritorial provisions**
- **Federal jurisdiction**
- **Methods for meeting employers' obligations**

Key Words and Phrases

United States Longshore and Harbor Workers' Compensation Act (LHWCA)

Jones Act (United States Merchant Marine Act of 1920)

Competitive state fund

Monopolistic state fund (exclusive state fund)

Employers mutual insurance company

Specific excess insurance

Review Questions

2-1. In addition to a state's workers compensation coverage being time limited outside the United States, what other problem should an insured be aware of?

2-2. Why do assigned risk plans for workers compensation insurance exist?

2-3. Aside from being created by a state legislature, explain how an employers mutual insurance company differs from any other mutual insurer.

Application Question

2-4. Exceptional Widgets is a small manufacturer with a dozen employees. The owner is considering retaining the risk of workers compensation losses.

a. What could a producer tell the owner of Exceptional Widgets about qualifying for self-insurance?

b. As an alternative to establishing a qualified self-insured plan to self-insure her company's workers compensation losses, the owner of Exceptional Widgets is also considering joining a self-insured group. What can a producer tell the owner about the advantages and disadvantages of a self-insured group?

Educational Objective 3

Summarize these sections of the Workers Compensation and Employers Liability Insurance Policy:

- **Information Page**
- **General Section**
- **Part One—Workers Compensation Insurance**

Key Word or Phrase

Workers Compensation and Employers Liability Insurance Policy (WC&EL policy)

Review Questions

3-1. Describe the information shown in Item 3 of the Information Page in a standard workers compensation and employers liability (WC&EL) policy.

3-2. Explain an insurer's payment obligations and legal requirements under Part One of the WC&EL policy.

3-3. Name four instances that would require an insured to reimburse an insurer for penalties required under a workers compensation law.

Application Questions

3-4. Sam works as a risk manager for the owner of a commercial building. He has requested and received the Information Page of an electrical contractor's WC&EL policy. Which items on the Information Page will Sam likely check and for what? For the purposes of this question please do not consider any endorsements such as being added as an additional insured.

3-5. Joanne is a chemical engineer who works at a large experimental facility that creates ways to improve the stability of plastic explosives, making them safer to transport. One day, Joanne used a mislabeled liquid solution that acted like acid when mixed with the other chemicals in her test tube. As a result, the solution exploded, leaving Joanne with third-degree burns over most of her body. The CEO of the facility withheld the information from the company's insurer, hoping that Joanne would accept his offer to "settle things quietly" to protect the company from an unfavorable public image. A few days later, Joanne died as a result of her injuries. Explain how Part One of the WC&EL policy will protect Joanne's dependents, regardless of the facility's misconduct.

Educational Objective 4

Explain why employers liability insurance is needed and how the Workers Compensation and Employers Liability Insurance Policy addresses this need.

Review Questions

4-1. Contrast workers compensation coverage with employers liability coverage.

4-2. Explain why employers need employers liability insurance in addition to workers compensation insurance.

4-3. Describe the three limits of liability that apply to employers liability coverage.

Application Questions

4-4. John is a car mechanic who works in a state listed in Item 3.A of the workers compensation and employers liability (WC&EL) Information Page. He drives to an unlisted state to buy the supplies he needs until his out-of-stock supplies are delivered. John is injured in an auto accident while in the unlisted state. Explain whether Part Two of the WC&EL policy will cover John's injuries.

4-5. Kim is a contractor who installs energy-efficient windows. She employs fifteen installers. A supplier of a popular brand of windows she installs required her to assume the supplier's liability for injury to her employees. Yesterday, two of her installers suffered severe lacerations while installing the supplier's windows. Kim is insured under a WC&EL policy and a Commercial General Liability (CGL) Coverage Form. Explain what coverage Kim has for this incident.

Educational Objective 5

Describe the purpose and operation of Part Three—Other States Insurance in the Workers Compensation and Employers Liability Insurance Policy.

Key Word or Phrase

Stop gap coverage

Review Questions

5-1. If an insured begins operations in a state designated in Item 3.C of the Information Page in the Workers Compensation & Employers Liability (WC&EL) Policy, what does the policy require the insured to do for the insurer?

5-2. If an insurer is licensed to write workers compensation insurance in all states, explain how the following Item 3.C wording protects the insured: "All states except those listed in Item 3.A and ND, OH, WA, and WY."

5-3. Explain the purpose of stopgap coverage.

Application Question

5-4. The owners of a bottled water distributor located and insured in a state listed in Item 3.A are considering expanding operations into three unlisted states. Explain their responsibilities if they decide to expand operations on the effective date of the policy and how the insurer differentiates between listing the states in Item 3.A or Item 3.C.

Educational Objective 6

Describe the need for and the coverage provided by each of the following endorsements:

- **Voluntary Compensation and Employers' Liability Coverage Endorsement**
- **Longshore and Harbor Workers' Compensation Act Coverage Endorsement**

Key Words and Phrases

Voluntary Compensation and Employers Liability Coverage Endorsement

United States Longshore and Harbor Workers' Compensation Act Endorsement

Review Questions

6-1. Identify occupations and situations commonly exempted from statutory workers compensation insurance.

6-2. Explain an insurer's obligations regarding compensation with a Voluntary Compensation and Employers Liability Endorsement.

6-3. Explain how the Longshore and Harbor Workers' Compensation Act (LHWCA) endorsement amends the definition of workers compensation law.

Application Question

6-4. Eriq and Liliana own Appleberry Farm. To protect their employees in the event of illness or injury, Eriq and Liliana purchased a Voluntary Compensation and Employers Liability Endorsement. John, a farmhand, was injured on the tractor while harvesting crops. John sued Appleberry Farm, stating that his complaints about the tractor's faulty emergency brake were ignored by Eriq and Liliana. Explain how the Voluntary Compensation and Employers Liability Endorsement will affect John's lawsuit.

Educational Objective 7
Explain how premium bases, classifications, and premium adjustments affect the rating of workers compensation insurance.

Key Words and Phrases

Experience modification

Retrospective rating plan

Large deductible plan

Review Questions

7-1. What is the purpose of the workers compensation classification system?

7-2. Explain why payroll is an effective premium base for workers compensation insurance.

7-3. Briefly explain how premium determined by applying the rates to the exposures (payroll) can be modified by the following workers compensation and employers liability (WC&EL) premium adjustments:

a. Premium discount

b. Merit or schedule rating factors

c. Rate deviations

d. Dividend plans

Application Question

7-4. The owner of West Coast Widget, a small manufacturing company, asked her insurance agent to explain several aspects of West Coast's workers compensation insurance.

a. West Coast Widget received one rating classification for all of its employees, although the work of some employees is more hazardous than that of others. Explain the classification system used in rating workers compensation insurance.

b. How would experience rating affect West Coast Widget's workers compensation insurance premium?

c. West Coast's owner is concerned about the high premium cost of workers compensation coverage, particularly in light of her employees' excellent safety record. She would prefer to self-insure but is uncertain about performing the administrative and claim adjusting functions in-house. Could her producer suggest an alternative?

Educational Objective 8

Given a case, determine whether the Workers Compensation and Employers Liability Insurance Policy covers a described injury or illness and, if so, what types of benefits or what amount of damages is covered.

Application Question

8-1. Carriboo Games (CG), based in Nevada, manufactures gaming equipment. On January 5, 20X1, CG began aggressively expanding its remote sales force, which included hiring Steve in Ohio to sell in that state. On January 10, 20X1, Steve was driving to a sales call when he was injured in an auto accident. He required hospitalization and weeks of rehabilitation before being able to return to work. Steve chose to file for workers compensation benefits under the Ohio statute.

CG is the named insured under a Workers Compensation and Employers Liability Insurance Policy (WC&EL policy) with an effective date of January 1, 20X1. At that time, Nevada was the only state listed in Item 3.A of CG's Information Page. CG's insurer is licensed to write workers compensation insurance in all states except those with monopolistic state funds. Item 3.C on the Information Page of CG's policy reads: "All except those listed in Item 3.A and ND, OH, WA, and WY." CG did not notify its insurer that it had begun hiring a remote sales force based in other states until Steve had his accident on January 10, 20X1.

a. Using Step 1: Declarations of the DICE method, does the declarations page, referred to as the Information Page of CG's WC&EL policy, support coverage for Steve's accident?

b. Using Step 2: Insuring Agreement of the DICE method, does the declarations page, referred to as the Information Page of CG's WC&EL policy, support coverage for Steve's accident if he chooses to file for workers compensation benefits under the Ohio statute?

c. Using Step 2: Insuring Agreement of the DICE method, does the Information Page of CG's WC&EL policy, support coverage for Steve's accident if he chooses to file for workers compensation benefits under the Nevada statute?

Answers to Assignment 9 Questions

NOTE: These answers are provided to give students a basic understanding of acceptable types of responses. They often are not the only valid answers and are not intended to provide an exhaustive response to the questions.

Educational Objective 1

1-1.   To be covered under a workers compensation statute, an injury or a disease must (in most states) arise out of and in the course of employment. That is, the injury or disease must be causally related to the employment and occur while the employee is engaged in work-related activities.

1-2.   These answers describe the benefits included:

   a.   In most instances, the workers compensation law provides full and unlimited medical expense benefits for a covered injury or disease. These benefits include medical, hospital, surgical, and other related medical care costs, including physical therapy and prosthetic devices.

   b.   Subject to a waiting period deductible, compensation for wage loss for a temporary partial disability, a temporary total disability, a permanent partial disability, or a permanent total disability is limited to a percentage of the employee's average weekly wage at the time of disability and is also subject to maximum and minimum weekly benefit amounts, which vary widely from state to state. State laws also require compensation for a specific number of weeks for the loss (or loss of use) of specific body parts. These injuries are referred to as "scheduled" injuries because the injuries and corresponding benefits are listed in a document called a schedule.

   c.   The primary rehabilitation benefit required is the payment of expenses for complete medical treatment and medical rehabilitation. Vocational rehabilitation may also be required by law.

   d.   Death benefits include a flat amount for burial expense and partial replacement of the worker's former weekly wage.

1-3.   The statutes of some states exempt employers with fewer than a stipulated number of employees, and many statutes specifically exclude certain employments such as farm labor, domestic workers, and casual employees. (A casual employee is one hired for only a short period, usually to accomplish a particular task.) Some employees are excluded because alternate plans are provided for them. For example, federal statutes govern the rights of various classes of employees to recover benefits or damages from their employers for occupational injury or disease. Examples of such classes of employees are federal government workers, maritime workers, and interstate railroad workers.

1-4.   It is important for a principal to verify that its independent contractors carry valid workers compensation insurance on their employees because if an independent contractor does not carry workers compensation insurance on its employees, the principal for whom the independent contractor is working may be held responsible for providing workers compensation to employees of the independent contractor.

1-5. Generally, Fran, as an employee, would be covered for any work-related injury sustained while at her place of employment or while traveling for her employer. Injuries occurring while traveling to or from work at a fixed location are typically not covered by a workers compensation statute. Fran was traveling to the training class where she was working that day, which would indicate she was not covered by her employer's policy. However, she was traveling for her employer while attending the training class in the bordering state and therefore workers compensation benefits are payable for her loss.

1-6. The temporary employment agency supplying the temporary employee provides workers compensation for temporary employees; the temporary employee is an employee of the providing firm, not the firm that is using his services. Therefore, the temporary employment agency's policy will respond to Steve's injury.

Educational Objective 2

2-1. In addition to time-limited coverage, another problem for firms with employees outside the country is that workers compensation laws in the U.S. may not provide coverage for repatriation expense or endemic disease.

2-2. Assigned risk plans exist to make insurance available. Some businesses cannot obtain private insurance in the voluntary market because they do not meet insurers' underwriting criteria. An employer rejected by private insurers can apply to the assigned risk plan in the appropriate state to obtain coverage.

2-3. An employers mutual insurance company closely resembles any other mutual insurer except that it is typically required by its charter to provide workers compensation insurance to any qualified employer in the state.

2-4. These answers address the Exceptional Widgets case:

a. To qualify as a self-insurer, an employer must post a surety bond with the workers compensation administrative agency of the state to guarantee the security of benefit payments. In addition, most states require evidence of an ability to administer the benefit payments and services mandated by the law. Self-insurance is usually practical only for employers with a large number of employees in a given state. Consequently, a producer may also advise the owner that Exceptional Widgets is not an ideal candidate for self-insurance.

b. Because they often deal directly with their members, self-insured groups claim that their costs for selling and servicing the coverage are lower than those of commercial insurers. However, in most states, self-insured groups are not covered by state guarantee funds. Therefore, to increase the comfort level of their members and to avoid catastrophically large losses, self-insured groups generally purchase excess insurance.

Educational Objective 3

3-1. Item 3 summarizes coverage provided by the policy. Item 3.A states that Part One—Workers Compensation Insurance applies to the workers compensation law of the state or states listed in that item. This space should list all states in which the insured has operations and the insurer is licensed to provide coverage. Item 3.B shows the limits of liability that apply to Part II—Employers Liability Coverage for bodily injury by accident and disease. Item 3.C indicates that Part III—Other States Insurance applies to any additional states listed under that item. Item 3.D can be filled in with a list of all endorsements and schedules attached to the policy at inception. In some cases, the endorsements are listed in a separate schedule attached to the policy.

3-2. The coverage provided by Part One obligates the insurer to pay all compensation and other benefits required of the insured by the workers compensation law or occupational disease law of any state listed in Item 3.A. of the Information Page.

3-3. The policy provides that the insured will reimburse the insurer for any penalties required under a workers compensation law in the following four instances:

- Willful misconduct

- Knowingly employing anyone illegally

- Failure to comply with health and safety laws and regulations

- Discrimination against employees who claim workers compensation benefits

3-4. Sam will check Item 1 to verify the electrical contractor is named on the policy as an insured. Sam will also check Item 2 to be sure the work performed by the contractor will be during the time the policy is in effect. He will also check Item 3 to confirm that the state where the work will be performed is in a state covered by the policy. Finally, Sam may check Item 4 to see if the contractor's work to be performed is properly described. If it is improperly described, the contractor's coverage may not be affected but it may give insight into who Sam has contracted with.

3-5. For the protection of the employee, the WC&EL policy provides that the obligations of the insurer will not be affected by the failure of the employer to comply with the policy requirements. The company's insurer will pay workers compensation benefits to Joanne's dependents. Since the contract is made primarily for the benefit of employees and their dependents, they have a direct right of action against the insurer.

Educational Objective 4

4-1. In contrast with Part One Workers Compensation Insurance, which covers an employer's liability under workers compensation statutes for occupational injury to employees, Part Two Employers Liability Insurance covers an employer against liability for an employee's occupational injury or disease that is not covered by a workers compensation statute. In addition, unlike workers compensation coverage, employers liability coverage is subject to monetary limits of liability stated in the policy.

4-2. Employers need employers liability insurance in addition to workers compensation insurance be-cause, depending on the laws of the particular state, an employer can still be held liable under the common law as the result of employee injuries, such as third-party claims or claims for care and loss of services.

4-3. These are the three limits of liability that apply to employers liability coverage:

- The bodily injury by accident limit is the most that the insurer will pay for bodily injury re-sulting from any one accident, regardless of the number of employees injured.

- The bodily injury by disease—policy limit is the most that the insurer will pay for bodily in-jury by disease, regardless of the number of employees who sustain disease.

- The bodily injury by disease—each employee limit is the most that the insurer will pay for bodily injury by disease to any one employee.

4-4. While Part Two requires that the employment out of which the injury arises be necessary or inci-dental to the insured's work in a state or territory listed in Item 3.A of the Information Page, it is not a requirement that the injury must occur in one of the states or territories listed. Even though John's injuries occurred outside of the listed state, the injury still arose out of employment that was necessary or incidental to the insured's work in a listed state. Therefore, Part Two of the WC&EL policy will cover John's injuries.

4-5. Employers liability coverage of Kim's WC&EL policy does not apply to liability assumed under contract—even when Kim assumed the window supplier's liability for injury to Kim's own employ-ees. Kim's CGL coverage form, by way of an exception to the employers liability exclusion in that form, covers Kim against liability assumed under an insured contract for injury to her employees. Otherwise, the CGL form excludes liability for injury to her employees.

Educational Objective 5

5-1. The policy states that the insured must "Tell us at once if you begin work in any state listed in Item 3.C of the Information Page."

5-2. If an insurer is licensed to write workers compensation insurance in all states, the wording used in Item 3.C often reads: "All states except those listed in Item 3.A and ND, OH, WA, and WY." This protects the insured if it commences operations in any state other than those listed in Item 3.A, which are already covered, or in any state other than the four monopolistic fund states, where it would be illegal for the insurer to provide workers compensation insurance.

5-3. If the insured anticipates operating in a state with a monopolistic workers compensation fund, the insured usually obtains workers compensation insurance from the appropriate state agency. Because the workers compensation policies issued by some monopolistic state funds do not include employers liability insurance, many employers buy a type of employers liability insurance called stopgap coverage.

5-4. If the distributor has operations in a particular state on the effective date of the policy but that state is not listed in Item 3.A, the owners must notify the insurer within thirty days or else no coverage will apply for that state. Thus, when operations are known to exist in a particular state, the insurer lists that state in Item 3.A. When operations do not currently take place in additional states but could be extended into those states, the insurer lists those states in Item 3.C.

Educational Objective 6

6-1. The occupations and situations most commonly exempted from statutory workers compensation insurance are farm labor, domestic employment, and casual labor. In some cases, the law does not apply to employers with fewer than a certain minimum number of employees. In addition, the workers compensation laws of some states do not apply to partners, sole proprietors, or executive officers.

6-2. The Voluntary Compensation and Employers Liability Endorsement, called "voluntary compensation," obligates the insurer to pay, on behalf of the insured, an amount equal to the compensation benefits that would be payable to such employees if they were subject to the workers compensation law designated in the endorsement.

6-3. The LHWCA endorsement amends the definition of workers compensation law to include the LHWCA with respect to operations in any state designated in the endorsement's schedule.

6-4. The voluntary compensation endorsement states that if an employee entitled to payment under the endorsement brings a suit under the common law, the coverage provided by the endorsement reverts to employers liability insurance. The insurer will defend the insured against the employee's suit and pay any settlement awarded, subject to the stipulated limits of liability.

Educational Objective 7

7-1. The class rating system serves to identify groups of similar employments, in terms of risk of injury or disease, whose experience is then combined for the purpose of establishing rates.

7-2. Payroll serves as an effective premium base because it varies directly with the exposure covered by the insurance, it is relatively easy to determine and verify from available records, and it is not readily subject to manipulation by the insured.

7-3. These answers address how the premium can be modified:

a. Many of the expenses of providing workers compensation insurance do not increase proportionately with increases in premium. For example, the costs of policy issuance and premium collection generally do not increase with the size of the premium. Also, the percentage paid to producers as a commission is usually reduced as the premium increases. In recognition of these lowered expenses, the premium discount plan provides an increasing credit for premiums in excess of a certain minimum.

b. In many states, the premium can also be modified by a merit or schedule rating factor to give the insured credit for conditions that are more favorable than those normally expected, such as superior housekeeping (standards that foster workplace safety), excellent employee training, and on-site medical facilities.

c. In some states, insurers are permitted to apply a rate deviation factor (for example, 10 percent) to the premium as calculated by the rating manual. Insurers generally reserve these credits for better risks, although competitive pressures sometimes result in average risks receiving a rate deviation.

   d. For policies written on a dividend plan, the cost of the insurance can be reduced by dividends declared by the insurer. Dividends are, essentially, a return to the insured of a portion of the premiums paid for an expiring policy term. Two general types of dividend plans are available: a flat-dividend plan and a sliding-scale dividend plan. Under a flat dividend plan, all eligible policies receive the same percentage of their premium as a dividend regardless of their individual loss experience. Under a sliding-scale dividend plan, the size of the dividend varies with the insured's own experience; the lower the insured's loss ratio, the higher the dividend percentage.

7-4. These answers apply to the West Coast Widget case:

   a. The classification system used in rating workers compensation insurance identifies groups of similar employments and combines their experience to establish rates. The insurer must determine the basic classification that best describes West Coast's business within the state. Then West Coast's exposure base and loss experience can be pooled with similar businesses.

   b. With experience rating, West Coast's premium for workers compensation insurance would be adjusted for a future period based on West Coast's loss experience for a recent period. For example, West Coast's premium for 2008 might be adjusted based on West Coast's loss experience for 2004, 2005, and 2006. The premium for 2008 would be reduced if West Coast's losses for 2004, 2005, and 2006 were less than the average for the class and increased if West Coast's losses were higher.

   c. Yes, West Coast Widget is a candidate for a workers compensation large deductible plan. A large deductible plan allows the insured to self-insure most of its workers compensation claims without establishing a qualifying self-insurance plan. Large deductible plans greatly reduce the premium and are available in most states. The insurer does all the administrative work connected with workers compensation claims, and the insured reimburses the insurer for claim payments up to the deductible amount per occurrence.

Educational Objective 8

8-1. These answers apply to the CG WC&EL case:

   a. The first DICE step is to review CG's Information Page to confirm that CG is the insured and that Steve's injury occurred during the policy period. CG did purchase the coverage and is the named insured. Furthermore, the policy was purchased on January 1, 20X1, and the accident occurred on January 10, 20X1, which was during the policy period. So the Information Page does support coverage for Steve's injuries.

   b. The second DICE step is to review the insuring agreement to determine whether it is applicable to the described claim. The coverage provided by Part One—Workers Compensation Insurance obligates CG's insurer to pay all compensation and other benefits required of CG by the workers compensation law or occupational disease law of the state listed in Item 3.A of the Information Page, which is Nevada. However, Steve has made a claim with CG for benefits payable under the workers compensation statute of Ohio, which is not listed as one of the states whose law applies.

Ohio is not listed in Item 3.A of CG's Information Page. That fact, by itself, will not prevent CG's policy from covering CG's obligation to pay Ohio workers compensation benefits to Steve. Part Three—Other States Insurance covers CG's obligations to pay benefits under another state's workers compensation statute if these requirements are met:

- Ohio is one of the states listed in Item 3.C of the Information Page.

- CG began its work in Ohio after the effective date of the policy and is not otherwise insured or self-insured for this work.

The first requirement is not met because Item 3.C of CG's Information Page includes all states except Nevada and the four states with monopolistic state funds, which include Ohio. Discussion of the second requirement, steps three and four of the DICE method, and determination of amounts payable do not appear to be necessary.

c. If Steve were to change his mind and file for benefits in Nevada, instead of Ohio, Step 2: Insuring Agreement of the DICE method, does support coverage since that state is listed in Item 3.A of the Information Page.

Direct Your Learning

Businessowners and Farm Insurance

Educational Objectives

After learning the content of this assignment, you should be able to:

1. Describe the typical businessowners policy (BOP) in terms of these elements:

   - The categories of loss exposures that can be covered by a BOP

   - The advantages of the BOP to insurers, producers, and insureds

   - Why BOP eligibility rules are necessary

   - How the BOP is rated

2. Contrast the property coverages of a typical businessowners policy with the commercial property coverages available in a commercial package policy.

3. Contrast the liability coverage of a typical businessowners policy with that of the Commercial General Liability Coverage Form.

4. Summarize coverages provided by the ISO farm program and how specialty farm coverages help farmers address additional loss exposures.

Outline

▶ **Overview of the Businessowners Policy**
  A. Loss Exposures Covered by the BOP
  B. Advantages of the BOP
  C. The Need for BOP Eligibility Rules
  D. Rating the BOP

▶ **Businessowners Property Coverage**
  A. Covered Causes of Loss and Valuation Provisions
  B. No Coinsurance
  C. Shorter List of Property Not Covered
  D. Automatic Seasonal Increase Provision
  E. Business Income and Extra Expense Coverage Included
  F. Other Property Coverages

▶ **Businessowners Liability Coverage**
  A. Limits of Insurance
  B. Professional Liability
  C. Hired and Nonowned Autos Liability
  D. Employee Benefits Liability and Employment Practices Liability
  E. Liability Coverage Options Generally Not Available in BOPs

▶ **Farm Insurance**
  A. ISO Farm Program
  B. Specialty Farm Coverages

Plan to take one week to complete each assignment in your course.

For each assignment, you should define or describe each of the Key Words and Phrases and answer each of the Review and Application Questions.

Educational Objective 1

Describe the typical businessowners policy (BOP) in terms of these elements:

- **The categories of loss exposures that can be covered by a BOP**
- **The advantages of the BOP to insurers, producers, and insureds**
- **Why BOP eligibility rules are necessary**
- **How the BOP is rated**

Key Word or Phrase

Adverse selection

Review Questions

1-1. What are the advantages of the businessowners policy (BOP) for insurers?

1-2. What are the advantages of the BOP for insureds?

1-3. Why are eligibility rules needed for BOPs?

1-4. Why is it much less complicated to rate property coverage under a BOP compared to equivalent coverages in a commercial package policy?

Educational Objective 2

Contrast the property coverages of a typical businessowners policy with the commercial property coverages available in a commercial package policy.

Review Questions

2-1. Contrast these provisions between most insurers' businessowners policy (BOP) and the Insurance Services Office, Inc. (ISO) commercial property program:

a. Covered causes of loss

b.   Valuation provisions

2-2. How does a typical BOP differ from the basic Building and Personal Property Coverage Form (BPP) with regard to property not covered?

2-3. How does the business income and extra expense coverage that is included in a BOP typically differ from the coverage provided by the Business Income (and Extra Expense) Coverage Form of commercial package policies with regard to each of the following?

a.   Coinsurance requirements

b.   Limits of insurance

2-4. Identify the coverages that would require separate policies or separate coverage parts in the commercial package program but that are frequently included as part of the BOP or available as options.

Application Question

2-5. Jeff and Chris own a small business on the Florida waterways called J&C's Tours. Jeff and Chris offer wildlife tours via passenger boats, which they operate. J&C's Tours conducts its operations from an office building and a floating dock that it owns. Assuming that J&C's Tours is eligible for a BOP policy, what advantages would the BOP offer in providing property coverage that the ISO commercial property program would not?

Educational Objective 3

Contrast the liability coverage of a typical businessowners policy with that of the Commercial General Liability Coverage Form.

Review Questions

3-1. Briefly describe these ways in which the businessowners policy (BOP) liability coverage typically differs from the standard occurrence version of the Insurance Services Office, Inc. (ISO) Commercial General Liability (CGL) Coverage Form.

a. Limits of insurance—limit amounts

b. Professional liability—availability of endorsements

c. Liability coverage options generally not available in BOPs

3-2. Explain why the availability of hired and nonowned autos liability coverage under the BOP offers an advantage to small insureds who own no automobiles.

3-3. How does an insured benefit from the ISO or American Association of Insurance Services (AAIS) BOP endorsement adding employee benefit liability coverage and employment practices liability?

Educational Objective 4

Summarize coverages provided by the ISO farm program and how specialty farm coverages help farmers address additional loss exposures.

Review Questions

4-1. Identify the property coverages used to insure residential buildings on a farm.

4-2. Contrast farm personal property Coverage E with farm personal property Coverage F.

4-3. Describe the four additional perils provided by the basic causes of loss in the farm policy.

4-4. Describe the coverage provided by crop-hail insurance policies.

Application Question

4-5. John owns and operates a farm where he grows soybeans and raises cattle. He and his family live in a house on the property, which also includes several outbuildings used for farming purposes. These buildings include a barn for the cattle and buildings used to store farm materials and equipment.

    a.   Which property coverages would be needed to cover the residential property on this farm?

    b.   Which property coverages would be appropriate for the farm outbuildings?

    c.   Explain why John might consider purchasing animal mortality insurance to cover his cattle.

Answers to Assignment 10 Questions

NOTE: These answers are provided to give students a basic understanding of acceptable types of responses. They often are not the only valid answers and are not intended to provide an exhaustive response to the questions.

Educational Objective 1

1-1.   Packaging several coverages in the BOP reduces adverse selection and, combined with simplified rating, lowers handling costs for insurers. Underwriting and processing policies through an automated system rather than through individual underwriting also reduces costs for insurers and enables the insurer and its products to compete.

1-2.   The BOP's advantages for insureds include convenience and economy gained from having one policy that meets most of their property and liability insurance needs.

1-3.   Eligibility rules are needed for BOPs because the rating structure of all BOPs contemplates a relatively homogeneous group of small to mid-size insureds. Writing BOP coverage for insureds that do not fall within this group can create a mismatch of premium and exposure.

1-4.   Rating a BOP is much less complicated because BOP property coverage is rated based on the amounts of coverage provided for building and personal property. BOP property rates include loadings (built-in charges) for business income and any additional coverages that are automatically included. As a result, the rates do not have to be computed separately for each of those coverages.

Educational Objective 2

2-1.   These answers contrast the provisions in most insurers' BOP and ISO's commercial property program:

a.   Most insurers offer only two versions of the BOP property coverage—a named perils form, similar to the commercial property broad form, and a special form. In contrast, the ISO commercial property program offers three causes of loss forms—basic, broad, and special.

b.   The standard valuation provision in BOPs is replacement cost, whereas the standard valuation provision in commercial property policies is actual cash value.

2-2.   In most BOPs, the list of property not covered is considerably shorter than the comparable list of property not covered in the BPP.

2-3.   These answers explain how the BOP's business income and extra expense coverage differs from the coverage provided by the Business Income (and Extra Expense) Coverage Form:

a.   In contrast to the Business Income (and Extra Expense) Coverage Form, the business income and extra expense coverage under the BOP is usually not subject to coinsurance, a monthly limitation, or even a total dollar limit.

b.   In contrast to the Business Income (and Extra Expense) Coverage Form, under a typical BOP, business income loss and extra expenses are payable for up to twelve consecutive months following the occurrence of the direct physical damage, and some BOPs limit ordinary payroll coverage to ninety days. Some insurers apply a dollar limit in addition to the twelve-month limitation.

2-4. These coverages would require separate policies or separate coverage parts in the commercial package program but are frequently included as part of the BOP or available as options:

- Employee dishonesty

- Money and securities, when special-form property coverage applies; or burglary and robbery, when named-perils property coverage applies

- Forgery

- Interior and exterior glass (if not included as part of the building and personal property coverage)

- Outdoor signs

- Mechanical breakdown

- Money orders and counterfeit money

- Computer coverage

- Accounts receivable

- Valuable papers and records

2-5. These advantages of the BOP would benefit J&C's Tours:

- Wharves and docks are not excluded by the BOP. Therefore, J&C's dock would be covered.

- Business income and extra expense coverage is automatically included. If the office or the dock were damaged by a covered peril, J&C's would incur extra expense to lease other office and dock space. This coverage could be especially important during a busy tourist season.

Educational Objective 3

3-1. The typical BOP liability coverage and the CGL coverage form differ in these ways:

a. BOP policies typically offer insureds fewer choices regarding limit amounts.

b. In many cases, BOPs can be endorsed to cover the professional liability exposures of specified insureds, such as pharmacies, barber shops, beauty shops, veterinary clinics, funeral homes, optical and hearing aid stores, and print shops.

c. Certain liability coverage options are not part of most BOP programs because the insureds that need them generally do not qualify for BOPs.

3-2. For an insured that owns no automobiles, the availability of hired and nonowned autos coverage under the BOP eliminates the need to obtain a separate business auto policy. If small insureds do not own any autos, they often overlook the need for, or cannot obtain, a separate policy covering hired and nonowned autos liability. Yet, almost every business at some time or another uses rented, leased, borrowed, or employee-owned autos.

3-3. The ISO and AAIS BOP endorsements adding employee benefits liability coverage and employment practices liability coverage are cost-effective options that enable smaller insureds to avoid the higher minimum premiums that usually apply to stand-alone policies.

Educational Objective 4

4-1. The Farm Dwellings, Appurtenant Structures and Household Personal Property Coverage Form contains four coverages:

- Coverage A —Dwellings

- Coverage B —Other Private Structures Appurtenant to Dwellings

- Coverage C — Household Personal Property

- Coverage D—Loss of Use

4-2. Coverage E—Scheduled Farm Personal Property applies to only those classes of farm personal property for which a specific limit of insurance is shown in the Declarations page. In addition to insuring specified classes of farm personal property, Coverage E can also be used to cover individually scheduled items of farm personal property, such as a particular tractor or combine owned by the insured. Coverage F—Unscheduled Farm Personal Property insures unscheduled farm personal property under a single limit.

4-3. The four additional perils are: theft, collision, earthquake (covering livestock only), and flood (livestock only). The collision peril has three aspects: collision damage to covered farm machinery, death of covered livestock resulting from contact with vehicles, and collision damage to other farm personal property. The earthquake and flood perils apply only to loss (by death) of covered livestock.

4-4. Crop-hail policies cover crop loss resulting from hail and are frequently extended to cover additional perils such as fire, windstorm accompanying hail, damage caused by livestock, and vehicles. Such policies may also cover harvested crops against named perils while being transported to the first place of storage.

4-5. These answers apply to John's farm operation:

a. The Farm Dwellings, Appurtenant Structures and Household Personal Property Coverage Form would cover the residential property. Coverage A would be used to cover the dwelling, and Coverage B would cover other private structures such as garages or sheds that are not used for farming purposes. Coverage C covers household personal property related to the dwelling.

b. To cover the barn and the storage buildings, John would need Farm Property—Barns, Outbuildings, and Other Farm Structures, Coverage G. This coverage insures all types of farm buildings other than the dwelling and other private structures appurtenant to the dwelling.

c. Livestock coverage provided by most farm policies is not adequate and normally covers loss of livestock only by specified causes. Animal mortality insurance is essentially term life insurance for animals and generally covers against loss of the insured animal by death resulting from accident, injury, sickness, or disease; or by theft, subject to exclusions.

Direct Your Learning

11

Specialty Coverages

Educational Objectives

After learning the content of this assignment, you should be able to:

1. Describe commercial excess liability insurance and commercial umbrella liability insurance in terms of these characteristics:

   - The three basic types of commercial excess liability insurance

   - The provisions commonly found in commercial umbrella liability policies that distinguish them from other types of commercial liability policies

2. Describe professional liability insurance and management liability insurance in terms of these aspects:

   - How they differ from each other

   - How they differ from commercial general liability policies

   - The common types of professional and management liability policies

3. Describe the purpose and characteristics of each of these types of environmental insurance policies:

   - Site-specific environmental impairment liability (EIL) policies

   - Underground storage tank compliance policies

   - Remediation stop-loss policies

   - Contractors pollution liability policies

   - Environmental professional errors and omissions liability policies

4. Describe aircraft insurance in terms of these characteristics:

   - The purpose-of-use categories that insurers use to classify aircraft

   - The coverages that can be included in an aircraft policy

5. Describe the types of losses that can be covered by each of the insuring agreements generally available in cyber risk insurance policies.

Educational Objectives, continued

6. Explain how an organization domiciled in the United States can insure foreign loss exposures that would not be covered under standard property and liability insurance policies.

7. Summarize the purpose and provisions of the terrorism endorsements developed by Insurance Services Office, Inc., and the National Council on Compensation Insurance, Inc.

8. Summarize the guarantee provided by the particular types of surety bonds within the following bond classifications:

    - Contract bonds

    - License and permit bonds

    - Public official bonds

    - Court bonds

    - Miscellaneous bonds

Outline

▶ **Commercial Excess and Umbrella Liability Insurance**
   A. Commercial Excess Liability Insurance
   B. Commercial Umbrella Liability Insurance
      1. Drop-Down Coverage
      2. Required Underlying Coverages
      3. Aggregate Limits
      4. Insuring Agreement
      5. Exclusions
      6. Conditions

▶ **Professional Liability and Management Liability Insurance**
   A. Distinguishing Between Professional and Management Liability
   B. Professional and Management Liability Contrasted With CGL
      1. Claims-Made Trigger
      2. Consent to Settle
      3. Duty to Defend and Selection of Defense Counsel
      4. Deductibles
   C. Professional Liability Policies
      1. Physicians Professional Liability Policies
      2. Insurance Agents and Brokers E&O Liability Policies
   D. Management Liability Policies
      1. Directors and Officers Liability Policies
      2. Employment Practices Liability Policies
      3. Fiduciary Liability Policies

▶ **Environmental Insurance**
   A. Site-Specific Environmental Impairment Liability Policies
   B. Underground Storage Tank Compliance Policies
   C. Remediation Stop-Loss Policies
   D. Contractors Pollution Liability Policies
   E. Environmental Professional E&O Liability Policies

▶ **Aircraft Insurance**
   A. Aircraft Liability Coverage
   B. Aircraft Hull Coverage
   C. Other Aircraft Coverages

▶ **Cyber Risk Insurance**
   A. Electronic Data Protection
   B. Cyber Extortion
   C. Cyber Crime
   D. Notification or Remediation
   E. Business Interruption
   F. Network Security Liability
   G. Privacy Liability
   H. Electronic Media Liability
   I. Technology Errors and Omissions Liability
   J. Intellectual Property Liability
   K. Terrorism Coverage

▶ **Insuring Foreign Operations**

▶ **Terrorism Endorsements for Commercial Property and Liability Forms**
   A. Disclosure Endorsements
   B. Cap Endorsements
   C. Certified Acts Exclusion Endorsements
   D. NBCR Exclusion Endorsements
   E. Limitations Endorsements
   F. Aggregate Limit Endorsements
   G. Punitive Damages Exclusion Endorsements
   H. Other Acts Exclusion Endorsements
   I. Auto Coverage Endorsements
   J. Workers Compensation Endorsements

▶ **Types of Surety Bonds**
   A. Contract Bonds
   B. License and Permit Bonds
   C. Public Official Bonds
   D. Court Bonds
   E. Miscellaneous Bonds

Narrow the focus of what you need to learn. Remember, the Educational Objectives are the foundation of the course, and the exam is based on these Educational Objectives.

For each assignment, you should define or describe each of the Key Words and Phrases and answer each of the Review and Application Questions.

Educational Objective 1

Describe commercial excess liability insurance and commercial umbrella liability insurance in terms of these characteristics:

- The three basic types of commercial excess liability insurance
- The provisions commonly found in commercial umbrella liability policies that distinguish them from other types of commercial liability policies

Key Words and Phrases

Excess liability policy

Umbrella liability policy

Self-insured retention (SIR)

Review Questions

1-1. Describe the three basic forms that an excess liability policy may take.

1-2. Explain why a self-contained excess policy might not cover a liability injury claim even though the underlying policy provides coverage.

1-3. What are the two functions performed by both umbrella liability policies and ordinary excess liability policies?

1-4. Describe the two types of claims in which drop-down coverage would apply.

1-5. Describe how an umbrella policy typically broadens coverage from that provided by an underlying policy.

Application Question

1-6. The Brownwell Company has an umbrella liability policy with a limit of $1 million and a self-insured retention (SIR) of $10,000. It also carries a business auto policy with a limit of $500,000. What dollar amount will Brownwell's umbrella insurer be obligated to pay for each of the following claims? Explain your answer.

a. One of Brownwell's employees caused an accident that is covered under both Brownwell's auto and umbrella policies. The injured party has been awarded $700,000 in damages from Brownwell.

b. One of Brownwell's employees committed a personal injury offense that was not covered by any of Brownwell's primary liability policies but was covered by Brownwell's umbrella policy. Brownwell was held liable for $160,000 in damages because of the personal injury.

c. One of Brownwell's employees caused an accident that is covered under both Brownwell's auto and umbrella policies. However, Brownwell has not maintained the business auto policy. The injured party has been awarded $800,000 in damages from Brownwell.

Educational Objective 2

Describe professional liability insurance and management liability insurance in terms of these aspects:

- **How they differ from each other**
- **How they differ from commercial general liability policies**
- **The common types of professional and management liability policies**

Key Words and Phrases

Professional liability insurance

Management liability insurance

Retroactive date

Extended reporting period (ERP)

Directors and officers (D&O) liability insurance

Entity coverage

Employment practices liability (EPL) insurance

Fiduciary liability insurance

Employee benefits liability insurance

Review Questions

2-1. Distinguish malpractice liability from errors and omissions professional liability.

2-2. Distinguish management liability from professional liability.

2-3. Explain why most insurers do not want to include professional liability coverage as part of the commercial general liability (CGL) coverage.

2-4. Why are claims-made policies used for professional and management liability?

2-5. Describe the professional liability policy provision known as the "hammer clause."

2-6. Describe the following insuring agreements contained in a typical directors and officers (D&O) policy:

a.   Coverage A

b.   Coverage B

c.   Coverage C

2-7. How does the Employee Retirement Income Security Act (ERISA) define fiduciary?

Application Questions

2-8. Dee, a physician, is insured under a professional liability policy. She misdiagnosed a patient's heart condition and subsequently prescribed the wrong medicine. In addition, Dee's nurse wrote out the prescription incorrectly, doubling the dose of the wrong medicine. The patient lost consciousness at home and was taken to the hospital, where he recovered. If the patient asserts a malpractice claim, which wrongful acts are covered?

2-9. Bill, a fifty-five-year-old employee of Ace Company, is fired despite a record of outstanding performance reviews. Bill believes he has been discriminated against because of his age and sues the directors of Ace Company. Describe the type of insurance policy that Ace Company would need to provide coverage for this type of lawsuit.

Educational Objective 3

Describe the purpose and characteristics of each of these types of environmental insurance policies:

- Site-specific environmental impairment liability (EIL) policies
- Underground storage tank compliance policies
- Remediation stop-loss policies
- Contractors pollution liability policies
- Environmental professional errors and omissions liability policies

Key Words and Phrases

Site-specific environmental impairment liability (EIL) policy

Underground storage tank (UST) compliance policy

Remediation stop-loss policy (cost cap policy)

Contractors pollution liability (CPL) policy

Review Questions

3-1. Describe what the insuring agreement in a typical site-specific environmental impairment liability (EIL) policy obligates the insurer to pay on behalf of the insured.

3-2. What two requirements can substantially restrict coverage under a site-specific EIL policy for claims alleging "cancer phobia" or similar fears of future disease or injury?

3-3. What are some of the exclusions commonly found in remediation stop-loss policies?

3-4. Who typically purchases environmental professional errors and omissions (E&O) liability policies?

Application Questions

3-5. Larry inherited two adjacent plots of land from his dad. He knew toxic waste had been dumped on the plots for several decades and that one plot is still leased to a waste management company. Neighbors of both plots are complaining of the pollutants' harmful health effects and are threatening to sue. Larry is seeking to purchase a site-specific EIL policy to respond to the threatened litigation. What potential problems could impair coverage that would normally be provided by an EIL policy, assuming Larry is successful in purchasing such a policy?

3-6. Verda is a contractor who performs environmental remediation services on contaminated sites. She is insured under a contractors pollution liability (CPL) policy. She recently bid on a job that, if awarded, would require her to perform asbestos abatement operations. Might she encounter a potential coverage problem if she is awarded this contract and, if so, is there a solution to the problem?

Educational Objective 4

Describe aircraft insurance in terms of these characteristics:

- **The purpose-of-use categories that insurers use to classify aircraft**
- **The coverages that can be included in an aircraft policy**

Key Word or Phrase

Aircraft insurance

Review Questions

4-1.   In addition to liability and physical damage, what coverages are often included in aircraft insurance policies?

4-2.   Describe the two most common aircraft hull coverages.

4-3.   Describe the types of deductibles under hull coverage for airplane insurance.

4-4.   For benefits to become payable under passenger voluntary settlement coverage what actions must be taken?

Application Questions

4-5. The company Vicki and Associates has purchased a single-engine high-performance aircraft. Vicki flies the plane as she travels for her consulting business. She keeps the plane in a hangar at a private runway owned by an association of professionals in her community. Describe the exposures that Vicki's company faces from the aircraft and the coverage available to address those loss exposures.

4-6. George purchased aircraft liability coverage. He employs Ralph in his business. George is flying his plane, with Ralph as his passenger, when a heavy suitcase falls out of an overhead bin, striking Ralph in the shoulder and causing an injury. How will George's aircraft liability coverage respond to this loss?

Educational Objective 5

Describe the types of losses that can be covered by each of the insuring agreements generally available in cyber risk insurance policies.

Key Words and Phrases

Intangible property

Denial-of-service attack

Malware

Infringement

Review Questions

5-1. Identify examples of additional terms used to describe cyber risk.

5-2. Describe the cyber risk insurance policies typically offered by insurers.

5-3. Explain why policies that offer first-party coverages have not been as widely available as those that include third-party coverages.

5-4. Describe the coverage a typical electronic data protection insuring agreement typically provides.

5-5. Describe the coverage a notification or remediation insuring agreement provides.

5-6. Describe the coverage a privacy liability insuring agreement typically provides.

5-7. Describe the coverage an intellectual property liability insuring agreement typically provides.

Educational Objective 6

Explain how an organization domiciled in the United States can insure foreign loss exposures that would not be covered under standard property and liability insurance policies.

Review Questions

6-1. List some of the specialized coverages that insurers offer to firms with foreign loss exposures.

6-2. What unique coverage is offered by many foreign voluntary workers compensation policies?

6-3. Admitted coverages available in many countries do not meet the needs of multinational enterprises. Explain how this problem is solved.

Application Question

6-4. Julia flew from her company's corporate headquarters in New York to Mexico City and rented a car to visit one of her company's suppliers. After her visit and dinner, the car Julia was driving hit and injured a pedestrian while she was en route to her hotel. Julia was found to be intoxicated and charged with the injuries to the pedestrian. Explain how Julia's company's business auto policy and its foreign supplemental and excess auto policy will respond to this loss.

Educational Objective 7

Summarize the purpose and provisions of the terrorism endorsements developed by Insurance Services Office, Inc., and the National Council on Compensation Insurance, Inc.

Review Questions

7-1. What three disclosures does the Terrorism Risk Insurance Act (TRIA) require insurers to make?

7-2. When should an insurer offer ISO-certified acts exclusion endorsements to an insured?

7-3. Must an insurer offer an ISO NBCR (nuclear, biological, chemical, or radio-logical) exclusion endorsement to all insureds? Explain your answer.

7-4. What is the purpose of an ISO aggregate limit endorsement?

7-5. What is the purpose of the terrorism endorsements developed by the National Council on Compensation Insurance (NCCI)?

Educational Objective 8

Summarize the guarantee provided by the particular types of surety bonds within the following bond classifications:

- **Contract bonds**
- **License and permit bonds**
- **Public official bonds**
- **Court bonds**
- **Miscellaneous bonds**

Key Words and Phrases

Principal

Obligee

Suretyship

Contract bond

Surety

Bid bond

Performance bond

Payment bond

Maintenance bond

Public official bond

Court bonds

Review Questions

8-1. Describe the two broad purposes of contract bonds.

8-2.   Describe the types of public officials who are commonly required by law to have public official bonds.

8-3.   Describe the guarantees provided by various license and permit bonds.

Application Question

8-4.   Robert, who designs and builds custom windows, is preparing a bid to provide windows for a refurbished office building in the town's historic district. He purchases special paned glass from Glass Supply Partners. Describe the various contract bonds Robert may be party to during this project, assuming his bid is accepted.

Answers to Assignment 11 Questions

NOTE: These answers are provided to give students a basic understanding of acceptable types of responses. They often are not the only valid answers and are not intended to provide an exhaustive response to the questions.

Educational Objective 1

1-1. The three basic forms of an excess liability policy are these:

- A "following form" subject to the same terms as the underlying policy

- A self-contained policy subject to its own terms only

- A combination of the first two types

1-2. A self-contained excess policy applies to a loss that exceeds the underlying limits only if the loss is also covered under the terms of the excess policy. For example, an excess policy may not cover injury within the products-completed operations hazard, even though the underlying policy does. In such a case, the excess policy would not pay for a products liability claim, even though the claim was covered by the underlying policy and exceeded the each occurrence limit of the underlying policy.

1-3. These are two functions performed by both umbrella liability policies and ordinary excess liability policies:

- Provide additional limits above the each occurrence limits of the insured's primary policies

- Take the place of the primary insurance when the primary aggregate limits are reduced or exhausted

1-4. Drop-down coverage is provided by many umbrella liability policies for these:

- Claims that are not covered by an underlying policy because the underlying policy's aggregate limits have been depleted

- Claims for which the underlying policies do not provide any coverage, regardless of aggregate limits

1-5. An umbrella policy typically broadens coverage from that provided by an underlying policy by using exclusions in the umbrella policy that have narrower application than the exclusions in the underlying policies. Another possibility is that the umbrella policy contains an exclusion that does not exist in any of the underlying policies and may provide narrower coverage than the underlying insurance for the particular exposure.

1-6. These answers concern Brownwell's insurer payments:

a. Brownwell's umbrella policy will pay $200,000. After the business auto policy pays its limit of $500,000, the umbrella policy will pay the amount of the claim in excess of $500,000. Because the primary coverage applies, the SIR is not applicable to this claim.

b. Brownwell's umbrella policy will pay $150,000. In this case, the SIR of $10,000 is deducted from the amount of the claim because the claim was not covered by any of Brownwell's primary policies.

c. Brownwell's umbrella policy will pay $300,000. Because the business auto policy lapsed and would have covered the first $500,000 in damages, the SIR does not apply. The umbrella policy applies as if the underlying insurance had been maintained.

Educational Objective 2

2-1. "Malpractice" is the term commonly used to describe liability associated with occupations that involve contact with the human body, ranging from beauticians to physicians. "Errors and omissions" is the term more likely to be used to describe professional liability for occupations such as accounting, insurance, law, and engineering.

2-2. Management liability is distinguished from professional liability in that it is less about individuals in occupations rendering or failing to render professional services and more about the wrongful acts of an organization or of individuals in their roles managing the operations of an organization.

2-3. Because professional liability requires different underwriting, rating, and claim handling skills, most insurers do not want to provide it as part of CGL coverage.

2-4. The reason for using a claims-made policy is that professional and management liability claims are sometimes not settled until long after the policy has expired.

2-5. Typically, professional liability and management liability policies provide that if the insured does not agree to a proposed settlement, the insured must take over the defense and pay any further defense expenses as well as the amount of any judgment or settlement that exceeds the amount for which the insurer could have settled the claim. This provision is sometimes informally referred to as a "hammer clause," because it usually compels the insured to agree to the settlement proposed by the insurer.

2-6. These are the insuring agreements contained in a typical D&O policy:

a. Coverage A—Covers the directors and officers of the insured corporation for their personal liability as directors or officers that results from a "wrongful act." Wrongful act is typically defined to include any breach of duty, neglect, error, misstatement, misleading statement, omission, or other act done or wrongfully attempted by the directors or officers.

b. Coverage B—Often referred to as company reimbursement coverage, it covers the sums that the insured corporation is required or permitted by law to pay to the directors and officers as indemnification for suits alleging wrongful acts by directors or officers.

c. Coverage C—For entity coverage, this covers claims made directly against a corporation (the entity) for wrongful acts.

2-7. ERISA defines a fiduciary as practically anyone whose role in employee benefits involves discretionary control or judgment in the design, administration, funding, or management of a benefit plan.

2-8. Both Dee's and her nurse's wrongful acts are likely covered by the professional liability policy. The misdiagnosis by Dee is a wrongful act that arose from improper performance in the practice of her profession as a medical doctor that resulted in the injury. Her nurse's wrongful act is also covered because Dee is legally responsible for her employee's acts while working under her supervision when rendering professional medical care.

2-9.   Ace Company would need an employment practices liability insurance policy to provide coverage for Bill's employment discrimination suit.

Educational Objective 3

3-1.   The insuring agreement in a typical site-specific EIL policy obligates the insurer to pay on behalf of the insured a loss, in excess of any deductible, for bodily injury, property damage, cleanup costs, and defense expenses.

3-2.   The first of two requirements that can substantially restrict coverage under a site-specific EIL policy for claims alleging fears of future disease or injury is that, for environmental coverage to apply, the bodily injury or property damage must result from pollutants emanating from an insured site. The second requirement is that physical injury or actual exposure to pollutants is required in some of the policy forms to trigger coverage for bodily injury claims.

3-3.   Some of the exclusions commonly found in remediation stop-loss policies are willful noncompliance with environmental regulations, bodily injury, contractual liability, and war.

3-4.   A wide range of professional environmental services vendors who face potential liability from professional errors, acts, or omissions purchase environmental professional E&O liability policies. Examples include environmental engineers, specialists from testing labs, tank testers, and environmental consultants.

3-5.   The first problem Larry faces in securing an EIL policy is that an exclusion exists for known pre-existing conditions. Coverage is excluded in situations in which the purchaser of the policy (in this case, Larry) knew of an impending claim that would be covered under the policy. The second problem is the exclusion for leased premises. EIL policies commonly exclude coverage for an insured location that the insured (in this case, Larry) has leased to another party (in this case, the waste management company).

3-6.   Yes, Verda will face a problem if she is awarded the job, for CPL policies often exclude the exposure of asbestos abatement operations. However, this exposure can often be covered by endorsement to the contractor's CPL policy.

Educational Objective 4

4-1.   In addition to liability and physical damage coverage, aircraft policies often include medical payments coverage, passenger voluntary settlement coverage (admitted liability coverage), and nonowned aircraft liability coverage.

4-2.   These are the two most common aircraft hull coverages:

- All risks—ground and flight, the broader of the two, covers the insured plane whether it is in flight or on the ground at the time of the loss.

- All risks—not in motion covers the insured plane only when it is on the ground and not moving under its own power. Thus, coverage applies while the plane is being towed, because it is not moving under its own power. Coverage does not apply, however, while the plane is taxiing, because the plane is moving under its own power.

4-3. Hull insurance on smaller aircraft is usually subject to a dollar deductible, either for a flat amount (such as $1,000) or for a stated percentage (such as 10 percent) of the plane's value. Some policies are written with a specified dollar deductible for ground coverage and a percentage deductible when the aircraft is in flight. Larger multiengine aircraft are sometimes insured with no deductible because deductibles do not eliminate many claims; the cost to repair even minor damage to such planes can amount to thousands of dollars.

4-4. For benefits to become payable under passenger voluntary settlement coverage, both of these actions must be taken:

- The insured must ask the insurer to pay.

- The claimant must release the insured from liability for all bodily injury caused by the accident.

4-5. Vicki and Associates' exposures from the aircraft and the coverages available to address those exposures are these:

- Physical damage to the aircraft—The aircraft hull coverage all risks—ground and flight will protect the plane in flight or on the ground.

- Bodily injury and property damage resulting from the ownership, maintenance, or use of the aircraft—Aircraft liability coverage will address coverage for liability to others, including bodily injury to passengers. Damage to the hanger may be excluded depending on the policy language used by the insurer.

- Medical payments losses for Vicki—Aircraft medical payments coverage will cover this exposure.

4-6. Ralph's injury is excluded because it involves bodily injury to an employee of the insured. In addition, the damages sought are likely to be similar to obligations payable under workers compensation or similar laws.

Educational Objective 5

5-1. Additional terms for this type of risk and the related loss exposures include e-commerce, cyber liability, Internet liability, cyber coverage (or insurance), and cyber security.

5-2. Insurers typically offer policies containing first-party-only coverage (property and theft), third-party-only coverage (liability), or both in a combination policy format.

5-3. Policies that offer first-party coverages have not been as widely available as those that include third-party coverages because first-party cyber risk losses can be difficult to assess and quantify.

5-4. An electronic data protection insuring agreement typically provides coverage for costs to recover or restore electronic data that have been altered, destroyed, deleted, or damaged.

5-5. A notification or remediation insuring agreement provides coverage for expenses related to crisis management during and after a cyber risk loss (typically related to a security breach).

5-6. A privacy liability insuring agreement provides coverage for liability arising from unauthorized disclosure or use of the private information of others or, depending on the insuring agreement, liability arising out of an insured's failure to comply with privacy provisions contained in laws such as the Health Insurance Portability and Accountability Act (HIPAA), the Gramm-Leach-Bliley Act (GLBA), or any anti-identity theft legislation.

5-7. An intellectual property liability insuring agreement provides an insured with coverage for any copyright, trade secrets, trademark, or patent infringement claims arising out of the use of the insured's protected ideas or works (or infringing on the protected ideas or works of another).

Educational Objective 6

6-1. For the needs of firms with foreign loss exposures, insurers offer these specialized coverages: foreign property and business income; foreign liability; foreign supplemental and excess auto; foreign voluntary workers compensation and employers liability; foreign crime, including kidnap and ransom, and political risk.

6-2. Foreign voluntary workers compensation policies often include coverage for transportation expense to return disabled or deceased employees to the United States ("repatriation expense").

6-3. To solve this problem, a multinational enterprise can purchase admitted coverages and combine them with a difference in conditions (DIC) policy written to wrap around the admitted coverages, thereby maintaining uniform coverage for all the insured's locations. In some cases, a global insurance program is purchased centrally from an insurer that can provide admitted coverage worldwide, either through its own subsidiaries or insurers with which it has reciprocal arrangements.

6-4. Julia's policies will respond to the loss in these ways:

- The business auto policy will cover losses only within the U.S. and its territories and possessions, Puerto Rico, and Canada. Therefore, no coverage applies.

- Foreign supplemental and excess auto policies are nonstandard forms. Assuming that coverage is extended by this policy to Mexico and to nonowned vehicles, this policy would respond to the loss.

Educational Objective 7

7-1. Insurance Services Office (ISO), Inc. disclosure endorsements present these TRIA-required disclosures:

- The portion of premium attributed to certified acts of terrorism

- The federal share of compensation for certified acts of terrorism

- The amount of the program cap

7-2. The insurer should offer ISO-certified acts exclusion endorsements when the insured has declined the insurer's offer of the TRIA coverage.

7-3. No. The insurer has the option of offering an ISO NBCR exclusion endorsement to an insured only when the insured initially rejects certified acts of terrorism coverage.

7-4. An ISO aggregate limit endorsement can be added to commercial liability coverage forms to limit the insurer's exposure and provide limited liability coverage for certified acts of terrorism for a reduced premium.

7-5. The NCCI's terrorism endorsements help insurers comply with the TRIA disclosure requirements and inform workers compensation policyholders about premiums related to acts of terrorism.

Educational Objective 8

8-1. Contract bonds serve these purposes: (1) The surety's willingness to furnish the bond is evidence that, in the surety's judgment, the principal is qualified to fulfill the terms of the contract, and (2) the surety guarantees that, even if the principal defaults, the obligations of the contract will be performed, or the surety will indemnify the obligee.

8-2. Officials required to obtain such public official bonds are those whose duties involve the handling of public funds, the seizure and disposition of property, the arrest or detention of persons, or any other duties that could result in violation of the rights of others.

8-3. License and permit bonds vary in what they guarantee. Some bonds guarantee compliance with laws that apply to the licensed activity; some additionally guarantee the payment of damages to anyone who suffers a loss resulting from noncompliance with those laws. Other such bonds apply to specific activities.

8-4. When Robert submits his bid, he may be required to furnish a bid bond guaranteeing that if the bid is accepted, he will enter into a contract to provide the windows. Once his bid is accepted, Robert will furnish a performance bond guaranteeing that he will complete the work according to specifications. As part of the contract with the building owner, he may also be asked to furnish a payment bond guaranteeing that he will pay Glass Supply Partners and any other suppliers and labor he uses for the project and a maintenance bond guaranteeing that the windows will be free of defects in materials and workmanship for a specific time after completion of the project.

Exam Information

About Institutes Exams

Exam questions are based on the Educational Objectives stated in the course guide and textbook. The exam is designed to measure whether you have met those Educational Objectives. The exam does not necessarily test every Educational Objective. It tests over a balanced sample of Educational Objectives.

How to Prepare for Institutes Exams

What can you do to prepare for an Institutes exam? Students who pass Institutes exams do the following:

▸ Use the assigned study materials. Focus your study on the Educational Objectives presented at the beginning of each course guide assignment. Thoroughly read the textbook and any other assigned materials, and then complete the course guide exercises. Choose a study method that best suits your needs; for example, participate in a traditional class, online class, or informal study group; or study on your own. Use The Institutes' SMART Study Aids (if available) for practice and review. If this course has an associated SMART Online Practice Exams product, you will find an access code on the inside back cover of this course guide. This access code allows you to print a full practice exam and to take additional online practice exams that will simulate an actual credentialing exam.

▸ Become familiar with the types of test questions asked on the exam. The practice exam in this course guide or in the SMART Online Practice Exams product will help you understand the different types of questions you will encounter on the exam.

▸ Maximize your test-taking time. Successful students use the sample exam in the course guide or in the SMART Online Practice Exams product to practice pacing themselves. Learning how to manage your time during the exam ensures that you will complete all of the test questions in the time allotted.

Types of Exam Questions

The exam for this course consists of objective questions of several types.

The Correct-Answer Type

In this type of question, the question stem is followed by four responses, one of which is absolutely correct. Select the *correct* answer.

> Which one of the following persons evaluates requests for insurance to determine which applicants are accepted and which are rejected?
>
> a.   The premium auditor
>
> b.   The loss control representative
>
> c.   The underwriter
>
> d.   The risk manager

The Best-Answer Type

In this type of question, the question stem is followed by four responses, only one of which is best, given the statement made or facts provided in the stem. Select the *best* answer.

> Several people within an insurer might be involved in determining whether an applicant for insurance is accepted. Which one of the following positions is primarily responsible for determining whether an applicant for insurance is accepted?
>
> a.   The loss control representative
>
> b.   The customer service representative
>
> c.   The underwriter
>
> d.   The premium auditor

The Incomplete-Statement or Sentence-Completion Type

In this type of question, the last part of the question stem consists of a portion of a statement rather than a direct question. Select the phrase that *correctly* or *best* completes the sentence.

Residual market plans designed for individuals who are unable to obtain insurance on their personal property in the voluntary market are called

a. VIN plans.

b. Self-insured retention plans.

c. Premium discount plans.

d. FAIR plans.

"All of the Above" Type

In this type of question, only one of the first three answers could be correct, or all three might be correct, in which case the best answer would be "All of the above." Read all the answers and select the *best* answer.

When a large commercial insured's policy is up for renewal, who is likely to provide input to the renewal decision process?

a. The underwriter

b. The loss control representative

c. The producer

d. All of the above

"All of the following, EXCEPT:" Type

In this type of question, responses include three correct answers and one answer that is incorrect or is clearly the least correct. Select the *incorrect* or *least correct* answer.

All of the following adjust insurance claims, EXCEPT:

a. Insurer claims representatives

b. Premium auditors

c. Producers

d. Independent adjusters